Hovenweep National Monument
Geologic Resource Evaluation Report

Natural Resource Report NPS/NRPC/GRD/NRR—2004/002

Geologic Resources Division
Natural Resource Program Center
P.O. Box 25287
Denver, Colorado 80225

September 2004

U.S. Department of the Interior
Washington, D.C.

The Natural Resource Publication series addresses natural resource topics that are of interest and applicability to a broad readership in the National Park Service and to others in the management of natural resources, including the scientific community, the public, and the NPS conservation and environmental constituencies. Manuscripts are peer-reviewed to ensure that the information is scientifically credible, technically accurate, appropriately written for the intended audience, and is designed and published in a professional manner.

Natural Resource Reports are the designated medium for disseminating high priority, current natural resource management information with managerial application. The series targets a general, diverse audience, and may contain NPS policy considerations or address sensitive issues of management applicability. Examples of the diverse array of reports published in this series include vital signs monitoring plans; "how to" resource management papers; proceedings of resource management workshops or conferences; annual reports of resource programs or divisions of the Natural Resource Program Center; resource action plans; fact sheets; and regularly-published newsletters.

Views and conclusions in this report are those of the authors and do not necessarily reflect policies of the National Park Service. Mention of trade names or commercial products does not constitute endorsement or recommendation for use by the National Park Service.

Printed copies of reports in these series may be produced in a limited quantity and they are only available as long as the supply lasts. This report is also available from the Geologic Resource Evaluation Program website (http://www2.nature.nps.gov/geology/inventory/ gre_publications) on the internet, or by sending a request to the address on the back cover. Please cite this publication as:

Thornberry-Ehrlich, T. 2004. Hovenweep National Monument Geologic Resource Evaluation Report. Natural Resource Report NPS/NRPC/GRD/NRR—2004/002. National Park Service, Denver, Colorado.

NPS D-35, September 2004

Table of Contents

List of Figures

Executive Summary

This report has been developed to accompany the digital geologic map derived from numerous published and unpublished geologic maps of the area covering Hovenweep National Monument in Utah. It contains information directed towards resource management and scientific research. National Park Service Geologic Resources Evaluation staff have assembled the digital geologic map that accompanies this report.

Although created to preserve the archaeological treasures left by the Anasazi, Hovenweep National Monument preserves much more than that. Like Mesa Verde National Park, Chaco Canyon National Historic Park and the other ancient Anasazi sites in the southwestern United States, Hovenweep illustrates the dynamic relationship and delicate balance between man and the environment around him.

In the late thirteenth century, this semi- arid region supported a vigorous agrarian population of over 2,500 Anasazi men, women and children as well as a thriving trade industry with other nearby groups. The single most important factor responsible for their survival, and probably for their migration away from the area, as well, was the geology. The Anasazi at Hovenweep called upon geological resources to sustain and maintain their culture.

Geology provides the foundation of the entire ecosystem. One stratigraphic unit of rock, the Dakota Sandstone, was the lifeblood of the Anasazi. The canyon rims upon which the Anasazi built their dwellings are Dakota Sandstone. The large, cohesive blocks of Dakota Sandstone that slumped onto the canyon floor also offered a foundation for some of the Anasazi's dwellings. Apparently, the stone used in constructing the dwellings and towers came from the Dakota Sandstone. Furthermore, the Dakota Sandstone was the source of their water, without which the area was useless to them. The Anasazi built their dwellings near the seeps and springs that emerged from the Dakota Sandstone at the head of canyons or at the contact with the underlying Burro Canyon Formation.

Understanding the geology of Hovenweep enhances one's understanding of the unique relationship between geology and their environment. In Hovenweep National Monument surface exposures consist primarily of Jurassic, Cretaceous, and Tertiary age rocks. In their record oceans came and went, deserts blew sand, and lakes and rivers passed through. Knowing the geology in detail is fundamental in determining the history of Hovenweep and in managing and preserving what is there today.

Geologic processes initiate complex responses that give rise to rock formations, surface and subsurface fluid movement, soil, and canyon formation. These processes develop a landscape that welcomes or discourages our use.

The preservation of the canyons, dwellings, dams, ledges, and assorted relics of Hovenweep National Monument is absolutely necessary to inspire wonder in visitors to the sites, and emphasis of geologic resources and the story of Anasazi culture with regards to them should be encouraged so as to enhance the visitor's experience.

The incredible ruins and desert landscape attracted over 32,817 visitors in the year 2002. These visitors are placing increasing demands on the resources available at Hovenweep National Monument. They were dazzled by the preserved dwellings, myriad of canyons and ledges, dams, castles, and towers. It is not surprising then that some of the principal geologic issues and concerns pertain to protecting these features. Humans have modified the landscape surrounding Hovenweep and consequently have modified its geologic system. This system is dynamic and capable of noticeable change within a human life span.

The following features, issues, and processes were identified as having the most geological importance and the highest level of management significance to the park:

- Erosion, seismicity, and preservation. The monument was created to preserve and protect some of the finest Anasazi ruins in the world. In the dynamic desert system, these features are at risk. Intense seasonal storms erode the canyons, undermining the foundations of the ruins. The region around Hovenweep National Monument is still seismically active making partial or total destruction of the ruins a concern.

- Slope failures and processes. Arid desert environments are especially susceptible to slumping and landslide problems during intense seasonal storms due to the lack of stabilizing plant growth. Road and trail construction also impacts the stability of a slope. Mudstone rich units such as the Mancos Shale and Morrison Formation are typically found in outcrop as slopes. These slopes are prone to fail when water saturated. In addition to this hazardous situation, the mudstones of the Morrison Formation are overlain by the cliff forming Burro Canyon Formation. This creates a situation in which the Burro Canyon is undercut, exposing large blocks of jointed sandstone to the force of gravity. Rockfall and slope failure is a potential almost everywhere these two units are exposed.

- Water Issues. Southern Utah receives on average only 8 to 10 inches of precipitation per year. This defines the semi- arid to arid climate that makes water such an important resource. Scant data exists regarding the capacity and hydrogeology of the system at the monument. This lack of information and monitoring makes managing the water resources at Hovenweep very difficult.

Other geologic parameters and issues such as swelling clays, uranium and other mining concerns, desert crusts, wind erosion and deposition, oil and gas exploration, paleontological resources, and air pollution, were also identified during scoping sessions as critical management issues for Hovenweep National Monument. These are detailed on pages 9- 12.

Introduction

The following section briefly describes the regional geologic setting and the National Park Service Geologic Resources Evaluation program.

Purpose of the Geologic Resources Evaluation Program

Geologic features and processes serve as the foundation of park ecosystems and an understanding of geologic resources yields important information needed for park decision making. The National Park Service Natural Resource Challenge, an action plan to advance the management and protection of park resources, has focused efforts to inventory the natural resources of parks. Ultimately, the inventory and monitoring of natural resources will become integral parts of park planning, operation and maintenance, visitor protection, and interpretation. The geologic component is carried out by the Geologic Resource Evaluation (GRE) Program administered by the NPS Geologic Resource Division. The goal of the GRE Program is to provide each of the identified 274 "Natural Area" parks with a digital geologic map, a geologic resource evaluation report, and a geologic bibliography. Each product is a tool to support the stewardship of park resources and each is designed to be user friendly to non- geoscientists.

The GRE teams hold scoping meetings at parks to review available data on the geology of a particular park and to discuss the specific geologic issues in the park. Park staff are afforded the opportunity to meet with the experts on the geology of their park. Scoping meetings are usually held in each park individually to expedite the process although some scoping meetings are multipark meetings for an entire Vital Signs Monitoring Network.

Bedrock and surficial geologic maps and information provide the foundation for studies of groundwater, geomorphology, soils, and environmental hazards. Geologic maps describe the underlying physical habitat of many natural systems and are an integral component of the physical inventories stipulated by the National Park Service (NPS) in its Natural Resources Inventory and Monitoring Guideline (NPS- 75) and the 1997 NPS Strategic Plan. The NPS Geologic Resources Evaluation (GRE) is a cooperative implementation of a systematic, comprehensive inventory of the geologic resources in National Park System units by the Geologic Resources Division, the Inventory and Monitoring (I&M) Program of the Natural Resource Information Division, the U.S. Geological Survey, and state geological surveys.

For additional information regarding the content of this report please refer to the Geologic Resources Division of the National Park Service, located in Denver, Colorado with up- to- date contact information at the following website:
http://www.nature.nps.gov/grd

Geologic Setting

Hovenweep National Monument consists of six clusters of ruins that straddle the Colorado/Utah border about 40 km (25 mi) north of the Four Corners. The 785 acre national monument was created by a proclamation from President Warren G. Harding on March 2, 1923. *Hovenweep* is a Paiute/Ute word for *deserted valley* but at one time (~500 A.D.), these desolate canyons and barren mesas of today's landscape echoed with the voices of over 2,500 Anasazi women, children, and men. Using local geological resources, the ancient architects built massive stone pueblos at the heads of canyons near springs and seeps emerging along the contact between geologic units.

Hovenweep National Monument is part of a much larger geological feature called the Colorado Plateau Province (figure 1). Covering parts of Colorado, Utah, Arizona, and New Mexico, the Colorado Plateau is a region of high plateaus and broad, rounded uplands separated by vast rangelands. The rangelands are underlain by large elliptical basins. The structural fabric of gently warped, rounded folds contrasts with the intense deformation and faulting of the terranes bordering the Colorado Plateau. Northeast and east of the Colorado Plateau are the jagged peaks of the Rocky Mountains. The Mesozoic- age Overthrust Belt marks the west- northwest edge of the Colorado Plateau. The extensional, normal- faulted Basin and Range Province that chopped the Overthrust Belt to pieces borders the Colorado Plateau to the west and south. The Rio Grande Rift, tearing a ragged scar in the landscape, forms the southeast border. Curiously, the Colorado Plateau remains somewhat of a tectonic mystery and has suffered relatively little geologic deformation compared to these surrounding regions.

The Colorado Plateau is also known for its laterally extensive monoclines (figure 1). The basins adjacent to the steep limbs of the monoclines have been filled with sediment eroded from these folds. These uplifts and basins formed as a result of the Upper Cretaceous- mid Tertiary Laramide Orogeny. The anticlinal Monument Upwarp lies to the west of Hovenweep National Monument and forms the western border to the Blanding Basin, a coincident synclinal downwarp. The rock layers, while gently folded into anticlines and synclines, remain relatively undisturbed by faulting except in areas associated with salt structures or dissolution of salt structures.

The La Sal Mountains and the Abajo Mountains lie north of Hovenweep National Monument, the Ute Mountains lie to the southeast, and the Carrizo Mountains are south, across the border into Arizona. These mountain ranges, as well as other mountains on the Colorado Plateau such as the La Plata, Rico, and Henry Mountains, are laccoliths, the results of hot, mobile magma material bulging up from deep within the earth. The splendid peaks of the San Juan Mountains to the east are the result of world- class volcanic eruptions

The giant monoclines, the laccoliths that dot the desert horizon, and other features present on the Colorado Plateau today were molded by the processes of erosion. The destructive forces of wind and rain, running water, and freezing temperatures attacked the uplifts and volcanoes relentlessly. The effects of erosion were probably negligible while the land lay very near sea level in the Early Tertiary Period. With a fairly abrupt increase in elevation from near sea level to several thousand feet above sea level in the Late Tertiary, however, the pace of erosion accelerated and attacked the Colorado Plateau and Rocky Mountain region with unprecedented vigor, carving the rocks and carrying away the dismantled strata to dissect the topography into the landscape we see today.

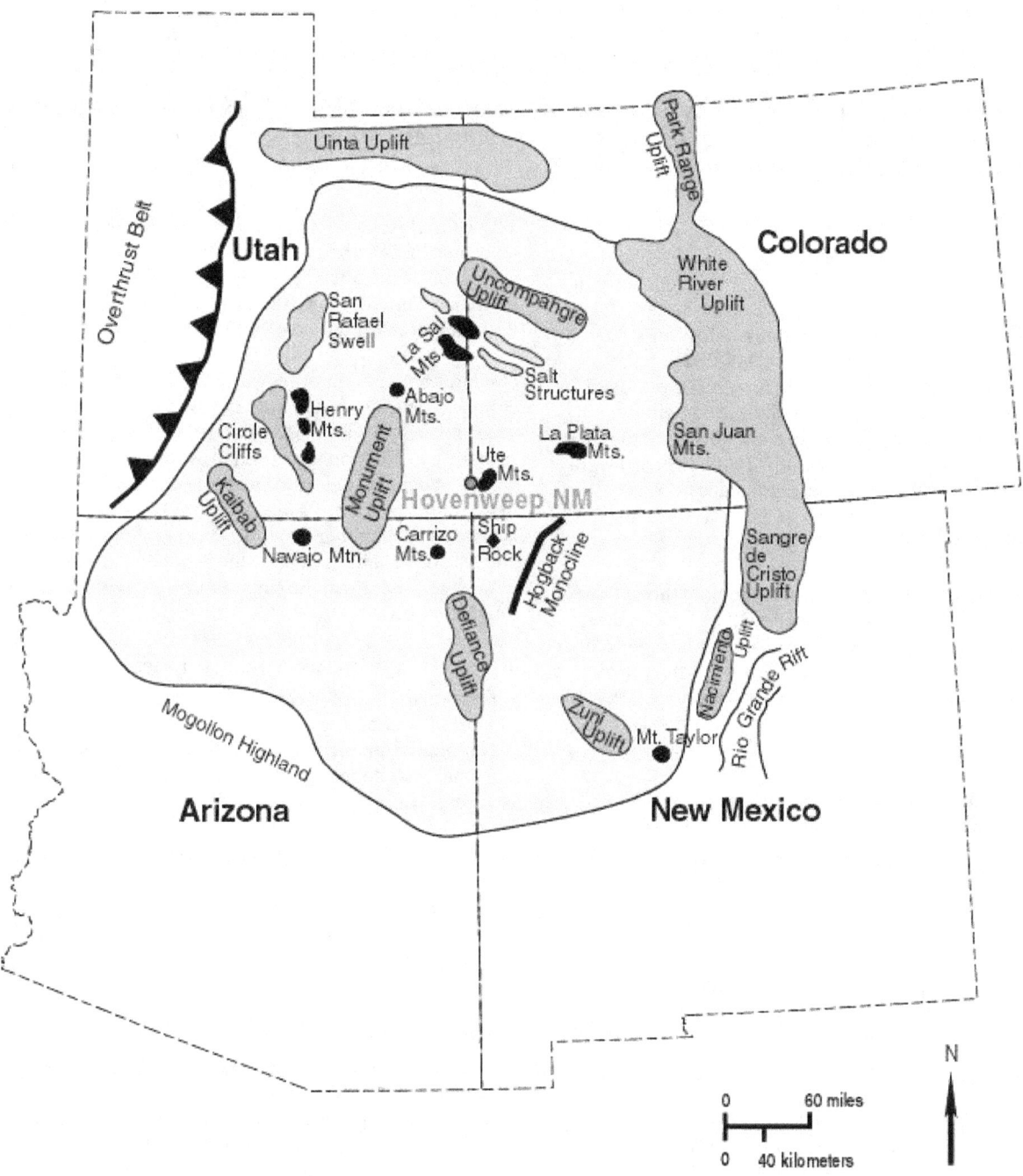

Figure 1: Location of Hovenweep National Monument relative to Colorado Plateau physiographic features. Light gray area signifies the areal extent of the Colorado Plateau. Dark gray and black areas represent uplifts and mountains.

Geologic Issues

A Geologic Resources Evaluation (GRE) workshop was held for Hovenweep National Monument from September 5- 6, 2000, to discuss the geologic resources, to address the status of geologic mapping by the Utah Geological Survey (UGS), and to assess resource management issues and needs. The following pages synthesize the results of this meeting to address economic resources, potential geological issues, future scientific research projects, and interpretive needs for Hovenweep National Monument.

Uranium and Mining Issues

The Paradox Basin has been the site of uranium mining for nearly nine decades. A discovery of a large unoxidized ore deposit on the flank of Lisbon Valley anticline, south of the monument, kindled public excitement in 1952 (Chenoweth, 1996). The principal host rocks for the radium, vanadium, and uranium deposits exposed at Hovenweep National Monument is the Jurassic Morrison Formation. In the Morrison, gray, poorly sorted, fine- to coarse- grained, calcareous, arkosic, quartz sandstone of the Salt Wash Member contains the uranium ore.

Abandoned mines pose a serious potential threat to any ecosystem. Even in arid environments, surface water, runoff, and groundwater can be contaminated with high concentrations of heavy metals, leached from the mine tailings. Heavy metals may also contaminate nearby soils which in turn can damage the plant and animal life that live on the soil.

Another threat specific to uranium mining is that of radon gas exposure. Radon is a daughter product of uranium radioactive decay and this tasteless, odorless gas is a known carcinogen that usually concentrates in low lying areas like basements and mine shafts.

Inventory, Monitoring, and/or Research Needs

- Conduct periodic water (surface and groundwater) and soil sampling and testing to detect uranium in those resources. Drinking water is especially important to monitor.

- Research needs include a thorough investigation of uranium bearing beds throughout the monument including descriptions, uranium content tests, and locations, i.e. where the beds crop out and are accessible to the public, flora and fauna.

- Complete inventory of the uranium content in the recent unconsolidated deposits and soils as well as the uranium bearing stratigraphic units (Morrison Formation)..

Slope Failures

Landslide and rockfall potential exists along all roads and trails at Hovenweep National Monument.

These events cause road problems and closures on a continual basis at the monument. Certain cliff forming units such as the Entrada and Dakota Sandstones, and the Burro Canyon Formation are especially hazardous when undercut by a road or trail.

Similarly, slumps and other forms of slope failure are common for units that are not necessarily associated with cliffs. Rocks rich in mudstone for instance, like the Morrison Formation are especially vulnerable to failure when exposed on a slope. The potential torrential rains necessary to produce flash flooding at Hovenweep also act as a sledgehammer on slopes lacking stabilizing plant and tree roots The rock and soil, suddenly saturated with water, slip down the slope causing a huge slump or mudslide/flow.

Inventory, Monitoring, and/or Research Needs

- Perform a comprehensive study of the erosion/weathering processes active at Hovenweep National Monument, taking into account rock formations, slope aspects, location and likelihood of instability.

- Create a rockfall susceptibility map using rock unit versus slope aspect in a GIS; use the map in determining future developments and current resource management including trails, buildings, and recreational use areas.

Erosion, Seismicity, and Preservation

The ancient Puebloans built their dwellings near springs and seeps. Groundwater percolated through the porous Dakota Sandstone until it encountered the impermeable shale of the Burro Canyon Formation. At this contact, the water was forced outward along the canyon walls. Dams were built to retain water and recharge groundwater. Today, these natural processes present a management challenge as they continue to undercut and erode the canyon walls and individual cultural units.

The Square Tower boulder foundation is eroding. A study of the problem and subsequent report was delivered to the Geologic Resources Division (GRD). A summary of that report is available on the HOVE website. Briefly, a consolidant was found that, when injected into the porous sandstone, slows the erosion process.

Earthquake potential is high along the Moab Fault in nearby Arches National Park, Southeast Utah Group (SEUG). While this and other faults in the Paradox Basin are associated with salt structures, the Colorado Plateau interior does possess a low level of seismic hazard (Wong *et al.*, 1996). Ground shaking from earthquakes may impact the ancient structures at Hovenweep National Monument causing catastrophic destruction.

Inventory, Monitoring, and/or Research Needs

- Use high resolution Global Positioning System (GPS) to detect moving, swelling, and collapse in areas of the monument.

- Obtain access to regular seismic activity reports or a seismometer to measure activity in the area.

- Perform a comprehensive, large scale, exhaustive map study of the canyons and buildings to determine minute points of susceptibility to failure and to better understand the structures and their weaknesses.

- Expand on the work that was done regarding the Square Tower unit, research that would carefully define the diagenetic history of the rocks and the cements that hold the grains together. A part of this study could incorporate the present effects of meteoric groundwater on the cement, pore space, and origin of diagenetic minerals.

Swelling Clays

Swelling soils associated with bentonitic shales of the Morrison, and Mancos Formations may be a concern to the present and future developments and management at Hovenweep National Monument. Bentonite, a clay derived from altered volcanic ash deposits, and is responsible for the road failures at Mesa Verde National Park among others. Bentonite has the ability to absorb large quantities of water into its structure so it will swell when wet and shrink upon drying, causing the ground surface to heave and buckle. Any structures, roads, trails, facilities, etc. found on soils with large concentrations of this mineral will be profoundly impacted and potentially destroyed.

This shrink- swell characteristic of bentonite produces interesting construction and road maintenance problems, but becomes a valuable property to the oil industry where bentonite is used to cool drilling bits and seal fractures.

Inventory, Monitoring, and/or Research Needs

- Use GIS to determine where trails, roads and buildings are present on bentonitic units. This method should also be employed to determine high risk areas where future development should be avoided.

- Perform an exhaustive mapping study of where specific bentonitic beds are located in the units listed above (Morrison Formation and Mancos Shale) to allow for more precise hazard assessment.

Paleontological Issues

The Geologic Resources Division of the National Park Service is conducting a separate paleontological inventory of the National Parks and Monuments so a detailed description of the paleontology and biostratigraphy of Hovenweep National Monument is beyond the scope of this inventory. The only report of paleontological resources from the monument is an unidentified bone found by Martha Hayden, a Utah Geological Survey geologist (Santucci, 2000). As has been noted, however, the Dakota Sandstone contains fossil pelecypod fauna. These and other invertebrate fossils are probably present in the monument, but no detailed study of the fossil material has been conducted.

Inventory, Monitoring, and/or Research Needs

- Research projects might be supported that would help identify the paleontological resources of the park as an aid to the GRD paleontological survey.

Water Issues

As true today as in the past, both surface water and groundwater play key roles in defining and shaping the Hovenweep landscape. Flowing water, however intermittent, helps carve the deep canyons, entrenched rivers, mesas, and spires that are so prevalent on the Colorado Plateau. Groundwater dissolves the cement that binds grains together and transports the cementing elements out of the system through seeps and springs. This erosion undercuts cliffs forming, alcoves, and rocks topple to the base of canyons. Water also expands as it freezes, pushing the grains apart, and when it thaws, the rocks collapse. In addition, the quality and quantity of water dictates biodiversity and the success of human occupation in an area.

The climate of Hovenweep is one of low precipitation and high evaporation rates. Consequently, recharge to groundwater aquifers is low. In the canyons, permeable Dakota sandstone overlies impermeable Burro Canyon shale and creates a favorable environment for seeps and springs. Water from rain and snow soaks into the sandstone but vertical flow is interrupted at the contact with the shale. The water is then forced outward, along the contact, and when it reaches the canyon wall, it forms a spring. Even in dry drainages, cottonwood trees in the canyon bottoms locate seeps and springs or areas where groundwater is near the surface.

All of these factors were taken into account when the Puebloan peoples settled the cluster of dwellings that became Hovenweep National Monument. Earthen dams, such as those at the Cajon ruins and near the remains of Hovenweep House in the Square Tower group, were constructed above springs in order to capture the precious water. Without the dams and with little vegetation to intercept the water, the rainfall and snowmelt quickly disperse as surface runoff. With the dams, the water collected in pools and slowly percolated downward to recharge the spring or slowly flow to garden plots.

The hydrology of the area may have served a spiritual, as well as a practical, role in ancient Puebloan culture. In contemporary Puebloan culture, springs are special locations associated with the creation of Puebloan peoples. Given the cultural significance of water at Hovenweep, it stands to reason that extensive study of the hydrogeologic system would lend to a deeper understanding of the interactions between landforms, water, and the inhabitants of the land. As yet, the system is poorly understood at Hovenweep.

Inventory, Monitoring, and/or Research Needs

- Conduct hydrogeologic studies to define subsurface flow patterns, regional and local flow systems, and the conductivity and transmissivity of the strata at Hovenweep.

- Monitor water quality on a multiple sample location basis within the monument, drinking water sources are especially important.

- Develop an understanding of groundwater and surface water flow in relation to erosion rates is critical to the survival of many of the dwellings at the monument.

- Define the hydrology of the area and of seeps along with the water quality, to establish a baseline for comparison. Water quality was mentioned at the workshop as a concern because of the numerous seeps along geologic units

- Install further wells for testing and drinking water access.

- Determine the impacts of copper and uranium mining and oil and gas drilling.

- Identify and study potential sources for groundwater quality impacts.

- Install transducers and dataloggers in wells.

- Investigate additional methods to characterize groundwater recharge areas and flow directions.

Desert Surface Crusts (biological and physiochemical) and Desert Pavements

Biological soil crusts composed of varying proportions of cyanobacteria, lichens, and mosses are important and widespread components of terrestrial ecosystems, and greatly benefit soil quality and ecosystem function. These plants increase water infiltration in some soil types, stabilize soils, fix atmospheric nitrogen for vascular plants, provide carbon to the interspaces between vegetation, secrete metals that stimulate plant growth, capture nutrient-carrying dust, and increase soil temperatures by decreasing surface albedo. They affect vegetation structure directly due to effects on soil stability, seedbed characteristics, and safe-site availability, and indirectly through effects on soil temperature and on water and nutrient availability.

Decreases in the abundance of biological soil crusts relative to physicochemical crusts can indicate increased susceptibility of soils to erosion and decreased functioning of other ecosystem processes associated with biological crusts. Physiochemical crusts can protect soils from wind erosion but not water erosion, and do not perform other ecological functions of biological crusts.

Inventory, Monitoring, and/or Research Needs

- Inventory condition and distribution of biological soil crusts.

- Investigate connection between ecosystem function and biological crusts.

- Map crust communities in relation to environmental factors.

- Study crust recovery rates and susceptibility to change.

- Study crust population dynamics and conditions.

Wind Erosion and Deposition

In addition to water, wind is a major force that can redistribute soil and soil resources (e.g., litter, organic matter, and nutrients) within and among ecosystems. Erosion and deposition by wind is important at Hovenweep and can be accelerated by human activities. Accelerated losses of soil and soil resources by erosion can indicate degradation of arid-land ecosystems because ecosystem health is dependent on the retention of these resources. In addition, wind erosion and sediment transport may be strongly impacted by land-use practices outside the parks. Eolian sand from disturbed surfaces may saltate onto undisturbed ground, burying and killing vegetation and/or biological soil crusts, or breaking biological soil crusts to expose more soil to erosion. Because park management practices limit or prohibit off-road travel, human impacts within the parks primarily are associated with off-trail hiking in high-use areas. Where livestock grazing or trailing is still permitted, accelerated soil erosion can be more extensive.

Inventory, Monitoring, and/or Research Needs

- Monitor movement of soil materials.

- Investigate impacts to the ecosystem of soil movement.

- Investigate natural range of variability of soil movement in relation to landscape configuration and characteristics.

General Geology and Interpretation

The unique geology of Hovenweep National Monument lends itself to potential scientific research projects that address the Mesozoic stratigraphy, the regional and local hydrology, and weathering/erosion rates.

Although the Mesozoic strata have been studied in detail in other locations on the Colorado Plateau, the strata at Hovenweep have not. Detailed descriptions of the depositional environments, the depositional systems, and the bounding unconformities are lacking. Furthermore, the flat-lying beds are deceptive. They overlie folded and faulted strata, and while seeming to represent passive, horizontal deposition, the surface layers are the signatures of dynamic tectonic processes resulting from a complex depositional and tectonic history.

The science of stratigraphy has undergone dramatic changes in the last twenty years and the strata at Hovenweep should be integrated into regional interpretations of the Jurassic and Cretaceous depositional regimes. Unconformities need to be identified and depositional environments defined on a bed-by-bed level of detail. The depositional environments, bounding unconformities, and depositional geometry of the Burro Canyon Formation and Dakota Sandstone need to be evaluated and integrated into a regional stratigraphic synthesis. The strata at Hovenweep are necessary pieces to this regional puzzle.

Inventory, Monitoring, and/or Research Needs

- Perform rock color studies.

- Identify unconformity-bounded stratigraphic packages in order to better define the depositional systems present in the past.

- Develop more graphics and brochures emphasizing geology, targeting the average enthusiast. Noted at the workshop was a need for a pamphlet or trail guide that describes the geology of Hovenweep National Monument for the visitor. Since geology is a strong component of the park, a geologic trail guide might enhance the visitor's experience.

- Develop an informative trail guide based on the detail GIS-NPS geologic map which has been published for Hovenweep National Monument. This would accent the strong geological component of the park and enhance the visitor's experience while at Hovenweep.

- Determine a timeline of canyon incision on the Colorado Plateau. The timing of canyon incision on the Colorado Plateau is an important topic of discussion among Quaternary geologists. Incision and erosion are directly related to weathering rates and regional tectonic regimes.

- Hire a full-time geologist to handle geologic issues for the SEUG.

Oil & Gas Issues

The combination of salt, organic-rich shale, porous limestone and sandstone, pressure and time has resulted in large accumulations of oil and gas in the Paradox Basin. Since the discovery of the giant Aneth Field in 1956, the Paradox Basin has been a prolific producer of oil and gas (Baars *et al.*, 1988).

The oil fields in southeastern Utah lie east of the Monument Upwarp in the vicinity of Hovenweep National Monument (Harr, 1996).

While not necessarily present within the monument, oil and gas accumulations surrounding the monument area pose a threat to the monument's viewshed and ecosystem. Geophysical exploration, the influx of drills, rigs and extraction equipment necessary for oil and gas production can create new road construction, water pollution, noise pollution and a localized population increase.

Inventory, Monitoring, and/or Research Needs

- Park staff should remain aware of the potential encroachment of oil and gas exploration in the area of the park.

- Acquire plugging records of oil and gas wells potentially connected to park groundwater systems.

Air Issues

Harmful chemicals and particulates are responsible for increased acid deposition in southern Utah. Sources of these dangers materials include the Navajo Power Plant, the Four Corners Plant, the Emery Plant and the Huntington Plant. Acid in the form of acid rain can dramatically affect the geologic landscape by preferentially eroding and weathering carbonate layers, intergranular cements and entire units of rock. This preferential erosion, accelerated by increase acidity of rainfall, can destabilize surfaces along slopes and cliffs causing significant hazards.

Inventory, Monitoring, and/or Research Needs

- Monitor rainwater pH, noting spikes or changes.

- Establish a working relationship with the appropriate industries in an attempt to decrease the level of pollutants in the area over the monument.

Geologic Features and Processes of Special Interest

Although present in the Hovenweep area from about 500 A.D., midway through the twelfth century, the Hovenweep Anasazi expanded their use of geologic resources and began building massive stone pueblos encircling the canyon heads. Nineteenth- century explorers referred to these structures as *castles* (Noble, 1991). Within the canyons, often below a spring, these people built tall stone towers that exhibit expert masonry skills and engineering. By the end of the thirteenth century, the Anasazi, including those at Hovenweep, mysteriously left the Four Corners region, never to return.

The square, oval, circular, and D- shaped towers at Hovenweep remain an enigma. Constructed with virtually no windows and in at least one case, without a door, the towers stand as timeless sentinels of a long-forgotten culture that thrived in the desert. Were they used as lookouts? Did they guard precious springs? Were they signal towers or used for celestial observations? Were they granaries or water reservoirs? Or, did Anasazi use them for ceremonies or general habitation? While some of the mysteries of the Anasazi remain, the foundation upon which the Anasazi built their culture at Hovenweep can be defined by looking at the geology.

The ruined castles and towers of Hovenweep National Monument are marvelously well preserved. Some of the best castles and towers are located in three canyons: 1) Square Tower Canyon, 2) Holly Canyon, and 3) Hackberry Canyon.

Square Tower Unit

The hydrology of the area, while allowing human habitation, is also responsible for the slow disintegration of the ancient ruins of Square Tower (figure 2). Spread along both sides of a Y- shaped canyon capped by Dakota Sandstone, the Square Tower Group contains the most concentrated remains of buildings at Hovenweep.

Square Tower itself is a three story high tower built on a slump block of Dakota Sandstone (figure 3). The sandstone is very porous, poorly cemented, and badly honeycombed with solution hollows along bedding planes. Consequently, weathering and erosion has caused some concern about the stability of Square Tower. A study conducted between 1991 and 1994 achieved some success at slowing erosion by using Conservare OH, a solution of ethyl silicate and methyl ethyl ketone. The solution absorbs into the pores of the rock and forms a silica gel cement. This process strengthens the bond between sand grains. Significantly, the solution does not completely fill the pore spaces and thus, water may continue to flow through the rock.

If water is trapped behind an impervious surface, spalling may occur. The solution also did not alter the appearance of the rock. Groundwater in samples did seem to inhibit the absorption of the consolidant, but if the solution was applied following a long dry spell, the rock may be strengthened without harming it aesthetically (Griffitts, 1994; www.nps.gov/hove/sqtower.htm).

While many of the ruins now grace the canyon rims, the canyons probably widened by rock collapse as groundwater and surface water undermined the soft Dakota sandstone. Hovenweep House (figure 4) and Hovenweep Castle (figure 5) now rest on the canyon rim and Tower Point is presently located at the center of the Y- shape of the canyon (figure 2). Hovenweep House is the largest ruin in the canyon and sits at the head of the South Fork. The ruins contain a multichambered, semicircular D- shaped tower. Hovenweep House is similar to Far View House on the Mesa Verde (Fewkes, 1919). Like other ruins, Hovenweep Castle has circular kivas embedded in rectangular rooms (figure 5). Tower Point appears to be a lone tower but the canyon was once filled with dwellings. As at Hovenweep Castle, buildings likely extended from the canyon bottom to the canyon rim at Tower Point. Stronghold House (figure 2) and Stronghold Tower were once connected by a log that bridged a crevice in the canyon. The slow, relentless process of canyon widening by slumping would have destroyed many of the dwellings and may impact the present structures in the future. Slump blocks and boulders also became building sites. Eroded Boulder House (figure 2) was constructed within a cave of a large boulder that came to rest below the canyon rim.

The Twin Towers (figure 6) overlook Eroded Boulder House from the canyon rim. These towers are a pair of two- story apartment- type buildings with sixteen rooms. In 1919, as today, the Twin Towers ruins ranked among the most impressive buildings in Square Tower Canyon (Fewkes, 1919). The towers stand on the south side of the canyon on a rock that is isolated by a cleft from the adjoining cliff. Small caves were walled up below the foundation on the northwest base of the larger room.

Unit- type House rests on the very edge of the canyon on the North Fork (figure 7) and is the simplest form of prehistoric pueblo (Fewkes, 1919). Rectangular rooms surround the centrally placed circular ceremonial room. The external form is oriented about due north. The central kiva sports exceptionally fine masonry and evidence of mural banquettes and pilasters to support the roof. The kiva with its vaulted roof is similar to Spruce- tree House, Cliff Palace, and Far View House on the Mesa Verde.

Horseshoe and Hackberry Units

Horseshoe House is located along the Canyon Rim Trail that connects Tower Point Ruin, Horseshoe House, and the Hackberry Site. The precision of the ancient architects and their use of natural products are magnificently displayed at Horseshoe House (figure 8). Each stone was carved to fit and mortar made from clay, sand, and ash, mixed with water from seeps in the canyon below was used to hold the stones in place. This mortar still holds the walls together, 800 years after they were constructed.

Hackberry Unit, as mentioned previously, may have had one of the largest populations of all the Hovenweep units because of its proximity to a constant seep of water. Archaeologists speculate that 250 to 350 people may have lived in the Hackberry Unit (www.nps.gov/hove/hshoe.htm).

Holly Unit

Located at the head of Keeley Canyon, the Holly Site includes Tilted Tower and Boulder House (figure 9). Tilted Tower is a multi-story pueblo built atop a large Dakota sandstone boulder. Processes of erosion and weathering caused the boulder to shift sometime after the canyon was abandoned (A.D. 1300). The upper stories of the tower tumbled into the canyon.

Boulder House (this may be Fewkes' Holly Tower, 1919) was also built on a Dakota Sandstone boulder, but in this case, the boulder is on the canyon bottom (figure 10). Like many towers at Hovenweep National Monument, Boulder House is located adjacent to a seep.

Cutthroat Unit

A breathtaking view awaits the visitor to Cutthroat Castle. Cajon Mesa stretches to the south towards the San Juan River and Carrizo Mountains. The buttes and towers of Monument Valley can be seen to the southwest and the volcanic spire of Shiprock in northwestern New Mexico pierces the sky to the southeast. This view was certainly not lost on the ancestral Puebloans who settled in this area.

The climate, elevation, and wind-blown dust gave rise to a soil that supported a forest of piñon and juniper trees. These provided the Puebloans with a variety of useful products. Piñon seeds are rich in calories and protein. Piñon sap or pitch waterproofs and seals baskets. Clothing and sandals can be made with shredded juniper bark. Trees were burned in fires and used as building materials. The tree rings give archeologists an accurate age date for many of the structures.

Like today, the soil also supported sagebrush. Sagebrush flowers, seeds, and leaves were all part of the prehistoric diets. Sagebrush is a good source of iron and Vitamin C and will kill intestinal parasites if eaten in larger amounts.

Quaternary uplift and erosion also played a role at Cutthroat Castle. Quartz pebbles from stream beds were used to make stone tools such as knives, scrapers, and projectile points.

Cajon Unit

About 80 to 100 people lived in the village that makes up the Cajon Unit. As with the other sites, erosion and weathering have taken their toll on the dwellings. The surviving structures are located around the head of a small canyon, but other buildings have fallen victim to canyon widening processes and have been reduced to rubble. Small cliff dwellings are protected under the ledge of one canyon wall. A tower with stones fitted to the undulations of three large boulders attest to the skill and determination of the architects and masons of Hovenweep and are reminiscent of the masonry at Navajo National Monument in northeastern Arizona.

Goodman Point

Except for Goodman Point, the ruins represent groups of farming communities with sophisticated stone masonry buildings on the northern edge of the Upper Sonoran Desert (NPS, 1990). On the desert, the location of the Anasazi communities was controlled by the geology and hydrogeology.

These Anasazi took advantage of the geology of the area by building at the head of draws and ravines where the strata produce springs and seeps. They manipulated and conserved the precipitation by building check dams and reservoirs in a region that is too dry for modern dry-farming methods (NPS, 1990).

Unlike the other Hovenweep sites, Goodman Point is not in a desert. Rather, it sits in the midst of modern dry land farms that produce pinto beans and winter wheat. The significance of Goodman Point lies in its sheer size and complexity. Anasazi communities in Montezuma Valley were contemporaries with the Mesa Verde Anasazi. Goodman Point was one of the largest prehistoric settlements in the valley, at least twice the size of Cliff Palace at Mesa Verde. The ruins represent the climax of the lifestyle of the Mesa Verde or Northern San Juan branch of the Anasazi.

Folds

During the Laramide orogeny, the last major mountain-building event to affect the Central Rocky Mountains, the Colorado Plateau was folded into broad arches and basins. Hovenweep is located on the gentle southwest-dipping slope of the Blanding Basin, one of these broad basins formed during the Laramide orogeny (Haynes *et al.*, 1972; Woodward, 1988). Structural contours drawn on the base of the Dakota Sandstone show the Blanding Basin as a northwest- southeast trending structural trough, plunging to the southeast, bordered by Laramide- age uplifts. The Monument Upwarp lies to the west and the Defiance Uplift to the south (figure 1) (Haynes *et al.*, 1972; Woodward, 1988).

Additional folds mapped on the eastern half of the Hovenweep geologic map appear to be younger than the Laramide structures, and may be associated with the processes that formed Ute Mountain and McElmo Dome, southeast of the Monument (Ekren and Houser, 1965). The anticlines and synclines on the geologic map are plunging folds trending east- west. The Aneth Anticline in the southwestern portion of the map is associated with the Aneth oil field that was developed farther to the west. Petroleum exploration wells mapped in association with the eastern plunge of the fold have all been dry. A portion of the Dove Creek Anticline enters the map area in the northeast corner of the map. Goodman Point lies between the McElmo Syncline and an unnamed anticline that has been mapped in the Dakota and Morrison Formations. The trace of each fold axis disappears beneath Quaternary alluvium.

A laccolithic igneous intrusion in the Tertiary formed the Ute Mountains. The McElmo Dome, north of the Ute Mountains, may also be of igneous origin (Ekren and Houser, 1965). An oil well drilled into the central part of the McElmo Dome bottomed in igneous rock that could be related to those at Ute Mountain. The primary difference between the two uplifts lies in the geometry of their satellite folds. Long, relatively narrow anticlines that plunge radially away from the central structure characterize the McElmo structure (a significant carbon dioxide producer). The Ute dome, on the other hand, is characterized by broad flexures that lose definition a short distance from the central part of the structure (Ekren and Houser, 1965).

The structural configuration of the McElmo Dome may also have resulted, in part, from salt movement. Movement of Pennsylvanian age salt deposits in the Paradox Formation is responsible for the extensive salt anticlines that form a northwest- southeast trend on the Colorado Plateau. Salt Valley in Arches National Park to the north formed when the salt- cored anticline dissolved and collapsed. The igneous rocks intruded into the Paradox Formation (Ekren and Houser, 1965).

Faults

Steeply dipping normal faults are associated with the Ute Mountains and McElmo Dome, but they are not prevalent at Hovenweep National Monument. South of the Goodman Point unit, on the southern edge of the map, two normal faults of little displacement are present (figure 11). Both fault traces are inferred, however, as are the geologic contacts. The northwest- southeast trending fault mapped in the Westwater Canyon member of the Morrison Formation drops down to the south whereas the east- west fault mapped in the Salt Wash member of the Morrison Formation has a hanging wall that has moved north relative to the footwall.

At the Naraguinnep Reservoir in the northeast corner of the map, an outcrop of Mancos Shale defines the footwall of a northeast- southwest trending fault within the House Creek Fault zone. The hanging wall has moved down to the north relative to the footwall and juxtaposed Mancos Shale against the older Dakota Sandstone. In the Hovenweep area, the House Creek Fault dies out to the west beneath Quaternary eolian deposits without offsetting the Dakota Sandstone. On a Precambrian basement lineament map, the northeast trending House Creek fault terminates at the juncture with a major northwest trending lineament just northwest of the Ute Mountains (Harr, 1996). During the Pennsylvanian, left- lateral, strike- slip movement occurred along the House Creek Fault.

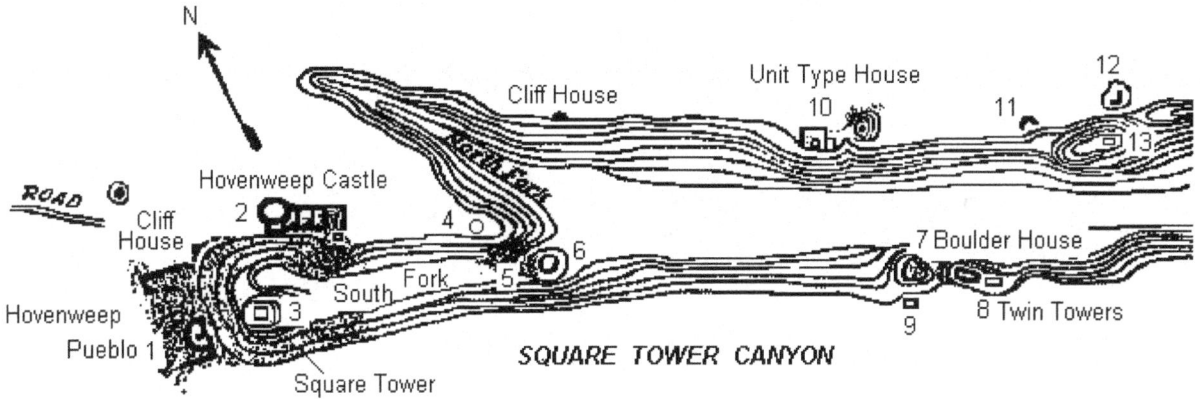

Figure 2: Ruins in Square Tower Canyon, Hovenweep National Monument, in 1919. Ruins: 1) Hovenweep House; 2) Hovenweep Castle; 3) Square Tower; 4) Tower Point; 5) tower walls rising from a ledge above the arroyo; 6) small tower at base of talus slope; 7) Eroded Boulder (Bowlder) House; 8) Twin Towers; 9) ruin walls; 10) Unit-Type House; 11) Stronghold House (cluster of several small buildings); 12) not described; 13) Stronghold Tower (?). Sketch from Fewkes, 1919.

Figure 3: Square Tower at Hovenweep National Monument built on a slump block of Dakota Sandstone. The sandstone is being eroded due to the presence of a nearby stream. The National Park Service built the stabilizing wall below the boulder in 1960. Photograph by Anne Poole, NPS.

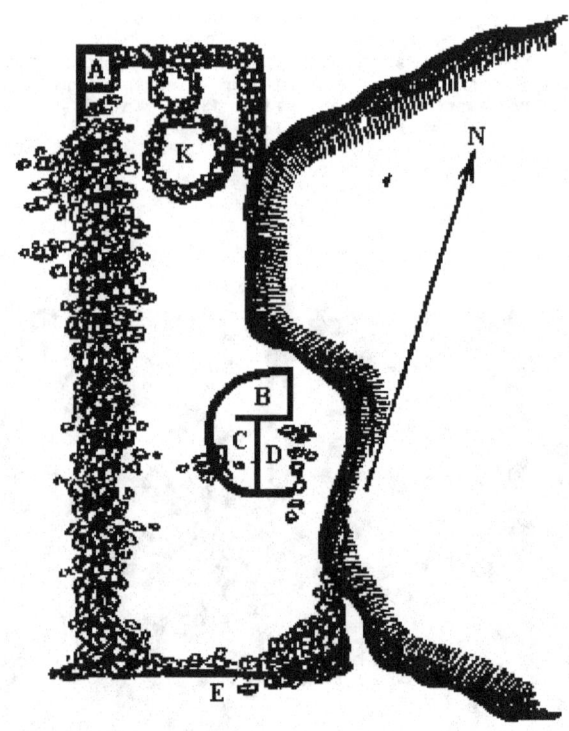

Hovenweep House

Figure 4: Ground plan of Hovenweep House, Square Tower Canyon, Hovenweep National Monument. High walls stand at the northwest angle of the ruin (A). Although walls have fallen, still remaining is a semicircle great house (B, C, D), kivas (K), and massive walls on the south side (E). Sketch from Fewkes, 1919.

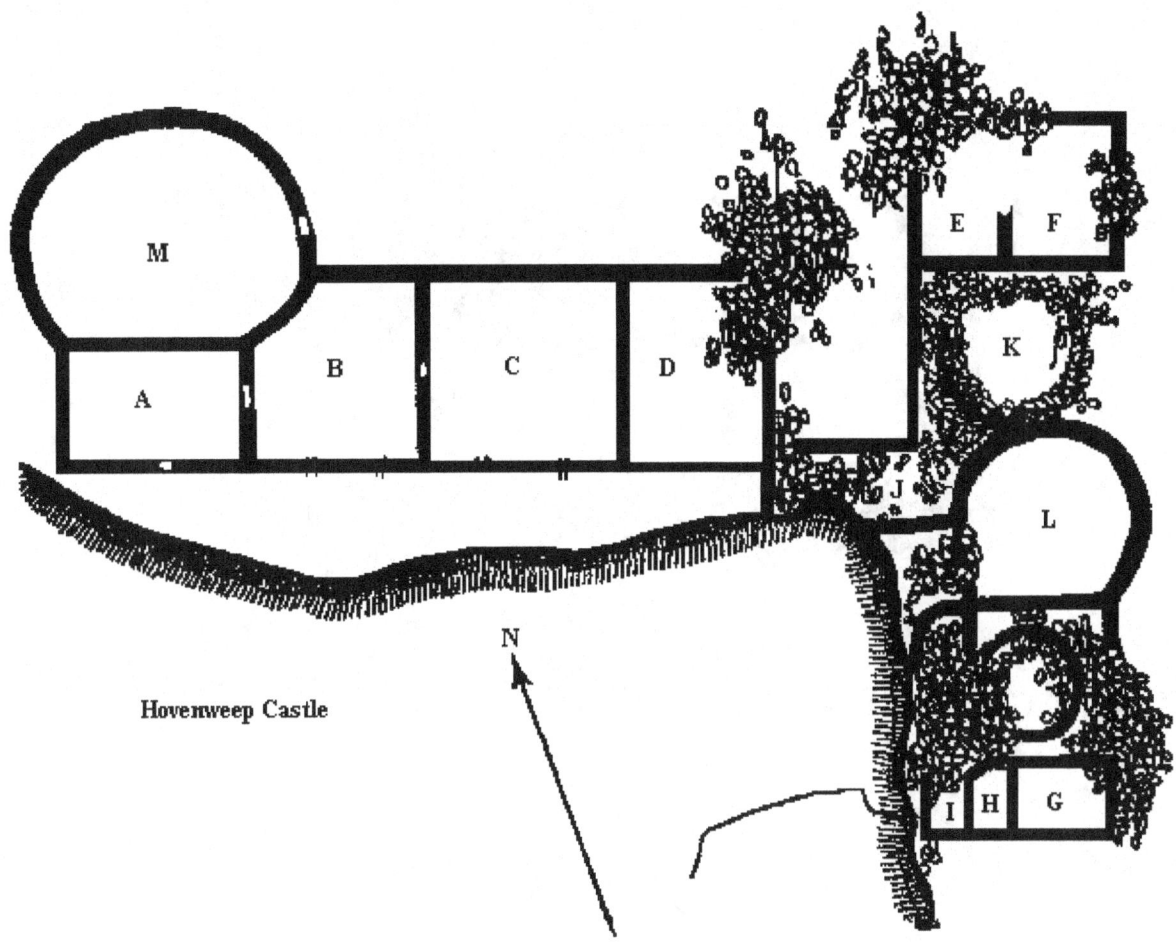

Figure 5: Ground plan of Hovenweep Castle, Square Towers Canyon, Hovenweep National Monument. Massive-walled semicircular towers (M, L) are connected in an L-shape by great houses and square rooms (A-I). Depressions indicate kivas (K). Sketch from Fewkes, 1919.

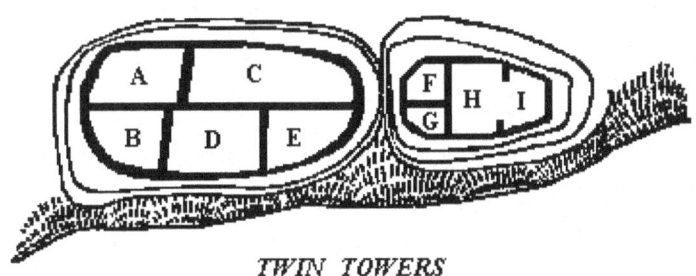

Figure 6: Ground plan of Twin Towers, Square Towers Canyon, Hovenweep National Monument. Letters A-I indicate rooms in the towers. Sketch from Fewkes, 1919.

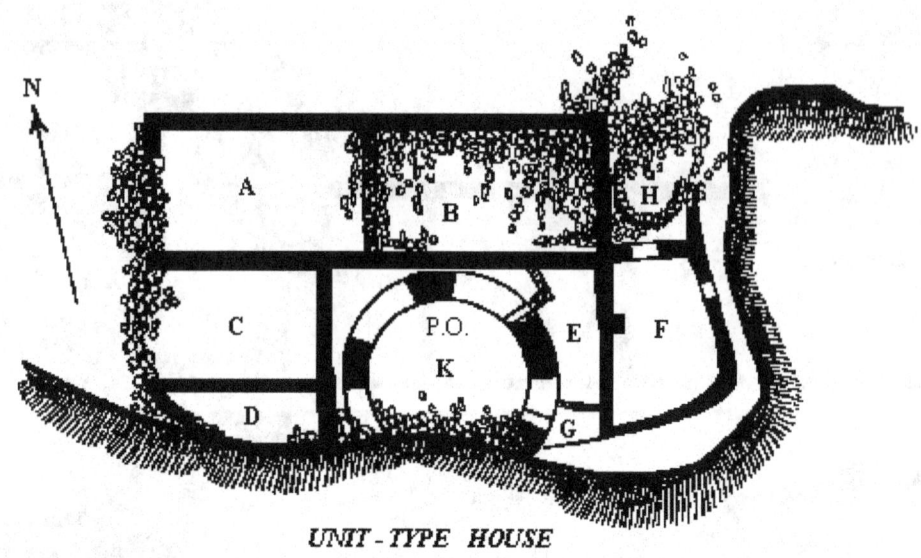

UNIT - TYPE HOUSE

Figure 7: Ground plan of Unit-Type House, Square Towers Canyon, Hovenweep National Monument. Rooms A-F clustered around a central kiva (K). A small room (G) may have held ceremonial objects. From Fewkes, 1919

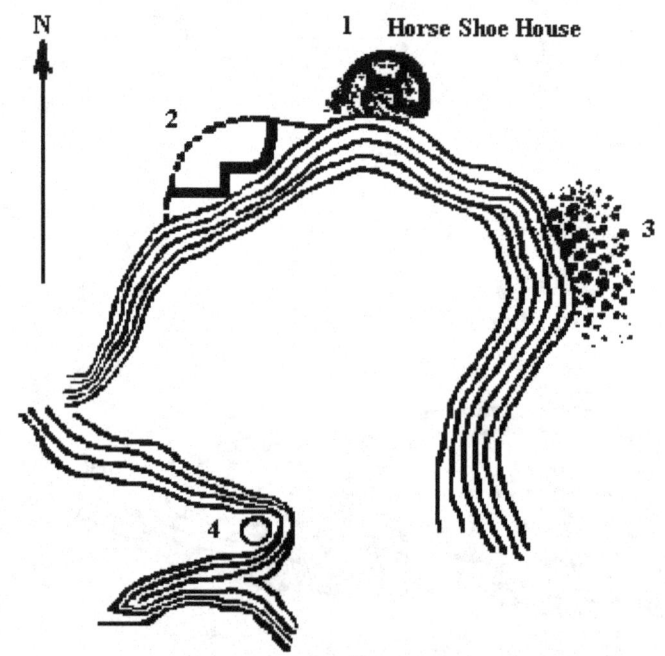

HORSESHOE (HACKBERRY) CANYON

Figure 8: Ground plan for Horseshoe House, Horseshoe (Hackberry) Canyon. A tower (4) stands on the canyon rim. Ruins (2, 3) are also on canyon rims. Sketch from Fewkes, 1919.

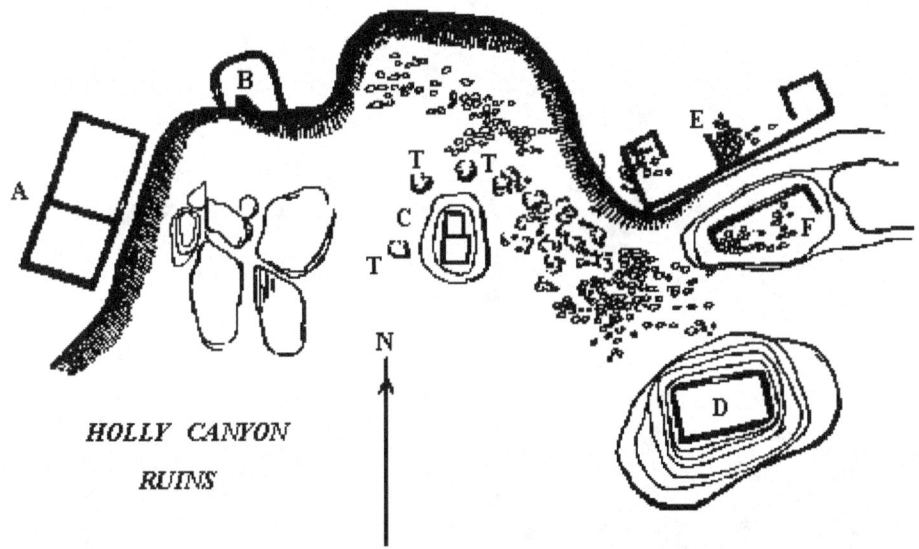

Figure 9: Ground plan of Holly Canyon Ruins, Holly Canyon, Hovenweep National Monument. Two towers (C, D) are constructed on fallen boulders. Ruins A and B stand on the rim of the canyon. Ruin A is the largest building of the group. The entrance to Ruin B may have been through the floor. Ruins E and F were once part of Holly House, a pueblo that was of considerable size. Sketch from Fewkes, 1919.

Figure 10: Holly Unit, Hovenweep National Monument. Dwelling is constructed on Dakota Sandstone that has subsequently been subjected to erosion, leaving the ruin in a precarious position. This is probably the ruin called "Holly Tower" in Fewkes, 1919, (figure 9, C). Photograph by Anne Poole, NPS.

Figure 11: Normal fault in East Rock Creek canyon (red line), north of Ute Dome and southwest of Goodman Point Unit, showing offset in the Entrada Sandstone (Je), Wanakah Formation (Jw), Junction Creek Sandstone (Jj), and the Salt Wash (Jms) and Westwater Canyon(Jmw) members of the Morrison Formation. Fault block on the left side of the fault has moved up (U) relative to the fault block to the right of the fault which has moved down (D). Photograph by Anne Poole, NPS.

Formation Properties

This section serves as a critical link between resource managers and the geologic map of the park. Formation Tables are highly generalized and for informational purposes only. Ground disturbing activities should not be permitted or denied on the basis of information contained in these tables. More detailed unit descriptions can be found in the help files accompanying the digital geologic map or by contacting the Geologic Resources Division at 303- 969- 2090.

The dwellings at Hovenweep National Monument are founded on the relatively flat- lying, Cretaceous- age Dakota Sandstone that caps the small canyons cut into the Cretaceous Dakota Sandstone and Burro Canyon formations and the Jurassic Morrison Formation and San Rafael Group (Hackman, 1955; Haynes *et al.*, 1972). Although mapped as a formation separate from the Morrison Formation on the geologic map (Appendix A, Attachment 1) (Haynes *et al.*, 1972), the Junction Creek Sandstone is now recognized as correlative to the Bluff Sandstone, a basal member of the Morrison (Peterson, 1994; Baars, 2000). The members of the Morrison Formation and the Cretaceous Dakota Sandstone and Burro Canyon Formation are the more prevalent rock units found in the monument, but the formations of the San Rafael Group are exposed in a canyon cut southwest of the Goodman Point ruins.

Between the deposition of the Mancos Shale and the unconsolidated deposits of recent, Quaternary valley fill and terrace deposits, approximately 80- 90 million years of earth history has been eroded from this landscape. Today, the Quaternary silts, sands, and gravels that are sparsely preserved in the canyons and surface depressions represent only a fraction of the deposits that once spread across this area only to be subsequently stripped from the Plateau by the relentless processes of uplift and erosion.

The following page presents a table view of the stratigraphic column and an itemized list of features per rock unit. This sheet includes several properties specific to each unit present in the stratigraphic column including: map symbol, name, description, resistance to erosion, suitability for development, hazards, potential paleontologic resources, cultural and mineral resources, potential karst issues, recreational use potential, and global significance.

Geologic History

Preserved Precambrian history began on the Colorado Plateau in the Proterozoic about 1,800 – 2,000 Ma when muddy sandstones (*graywacke*), shales, and volcanic rocks were deposited in a vast oceanic environment. Erupting volcanoes formed a chain of islands in this ocean beyond the southern edge of the North American craton (Reed *et al.*, 1987; Scott *et al.*, 2001). A period of compressive mountain building folded the Precambrian strata into tight, chevron- like folds and metamorphosed the rocks to gneisses about 1,740 Ma as the volcanic islands collided with the southern end of what is now Wyoming (Hutchinson, 1976; Tweto, 1980: Warner, 1980; Gregson, 1992; Scott *et al.*, 2001). Metamorphosed sedimentary rocks and volcanic rocks over 1,800 million years old are present in exposed terranes throughout Colorado and in the buried basement of the Colorado Plateau (Tweto, 1980).

Late Proterozoic rifting created a new continental margin along western North America. During the Late Precambrian through the Cambrian, thousands of feet of shallow- water, marine sediments accumulated along a passive plate- tectonic margin on the western side of the Transcontinental Arch, an upland that stretched from northern Minnesota southwestward across Nebraska, Colorado and northwestern New Mexico (Speed, 1983; Sloss, 1988).

Throughout the Paleozoic Era, Europe, Africa, and South America were approaching North America as the two great landmasses, Laurasia and Gondwana, collided. The ancient continent of Gondwana included Australia, Antarctica, Africa, South America, and India south of the Ganges River, plus smaller islands. Laurasia, located in the northern hemisphere, is the hypothetical continent that contained the present northern continents. These collectively formed the supercontinent *Pangaea* which was centered on the equator.

What happened geologically in the Ordovician Period (438- 505 Ma) and the Silurian Period (408- 438 Ma) in southwestern Colorado and southeastern Utah remains a mystery because no Ordovician rocks or Silurian rocks are present. The end of the Ordovician Period (438 Ma) is marked by one of the five most extensive mass extinctions of all time (see Figure 19). The other four occurred at the end of the Devonian Period, the end of the Permian Period, at the close of the Triassic, and of course, at the Cretaceous – Tertiary boundary.

By the beginning of the Devonian Period, the seas that had covered most of the continent had receded, or regressed, and the shoreline was far to the west. Tidal flats extended from western Colorado to central Utah. However, this quiet scene suddenly changed.

The first pulses of the Antler Orogeny in the west and the Acadian Orogeny in the east (part of the Appalachian Orogeny) began to be felt as landmasses accreted onto both the western and eastern borders of North America. To the west of Colorado, a subduction zone formed. As lithospheric plates collided against one another, their rocks were bent, folded, and thrust- faulted into a north-south trending mountain range stretching from Nevada to Canada. The Roberts Mountains Thrust marks the easternmost thrust sheets generated by the Antler Orogeny (figure 12).

By the end of the Devonian, great inland seas again covered the continent, and a sea inundated the area between the western mountains and Colorado (Johnson *et al.*, 1991). A marine carbonate platform extended into the Four- Corners area from the west. The Uncompahgre Arch, a feature that would eventually reemerge in the Pennsylvanian as part of the Ancestral Rocky Mountains, bordered the Four- Corners area to the northeast, and the broad Defiance Uplift lay to the southwest in New Mexico (Beus, 1980).

As the highlands to the west were thrust above sea level at the beginning of the Mississippian Period, southwest Colorado still lay about 5° south of the equator. The warm marine water gave rise to extensive deposits of carbonate rocks (figure 13). Limestone, and dolomitic mudstones deposited in the lowermost Mississippian Period reflect deposition in intertidal to restricted subtidal environments as the transgressive sea advanced from the west (De Voto, 1980A; Poole and Sandberg, 1991). The structural effects of compression on the western margin, however, could be felt as far inland as southwestern Colorado where local uplifts caused local regression and erosion. Aggressive tectonism in the Pennsylvanian Period built mountains (the Ancestral Rocky Mountains) in Colorado with as much as 3,000 m (10,000 ft) of relief (De Voto, 1980B). They supplied sediment to the Hovenweep area.

With increasing southwest to northeast- directed compression, a northwest- southeast trending, shallow, subsiding trough called the Paradox Basin formed across the Four- Corners area (figure 14) (Stone, 1986). Periodic marine incursions from the south flooded the Paradox Basin and record a history of marine transgression into the area. As the water evaporated, salt deposits (evaporites) formed. By Late Pennsylvanian time, the Paradox Basin had filled with evaporite deposits and the shoaling that developed eliminated any barriers to circulation. Near- normal marine conditions returned to the area, depositing marine carbonates (Rueger, 1996).

The Permian was a time of worldwide changing environments. In the area of Hovenweep, broad lowlands bordered an ocean to the west (Baars, 2000). To the east and northeast, however, the peaks of the Uncompahgre Mountains bordered the lowland.

The close of the Permian also brought the third, and most severe, major mass extinction of geologic time. The most recent hypothesis on the Permian event suggests that a comet, about 6-13 km (4-8 mi) in diameter, slammed into the earth (Becker *et al.*, 2001). The resulting atmospheric disturbance plunged the earth into an cooling trend with downpours of acid rain. Thousands of species of insects, reptiles, and amphibians died on land while in the oceans, coral formations vanished, as did snails, urchins, sea lilies, some fish, and the once-prolific trilobites. The catastrophe wiped out 300 million years of history.

In the Early Triassic (240 to 245 Ma), volcanic activity decreased on the western margin of the supercontinent (Christiansen *et al.*, 1994). The depositional environments in the Early Triassic represent a transition from marine and marginal marine environments in western Utah and Nevada to terrestrial (above sea level) environments in western Colorado. Throughout the Early Triassic the region around Hovenweep National Monument remained above sea level and *red beds* were deposited over the area. The red beds of the Lower Triassic, Moenkopi Formation were deposited in fluvial, mudflat, sabkha, and shallow marine environments (figure 15) (Stewart *et al.*, 1972A; Christiansen *et al.*, 1994; Doelling, 2000; Huntoon *et al.*, 2000).

The geologic history of the Middle Triassic remains a mystery in southwestern Colorado and Utah. No rocks that span this time range from 235-240 Ma have been preserved. The Upper Triassic is a different story. Continental rocks of the Western Interior form a complex assemblage of alluvial (river debris), marsh, lacustrine (lake), playa (dried lake), and eolian (wind) deposits (Stewart *et al.*, 1972B). Throughout the region, layers of bentonite (montmorillinite clays) formed from the alteration of volcanic ash, are interlayered with the clastic sediments. The bentonite layers indicate a period of renewed volcanism to the west (Christiansen *et al.*, 1994). As Pangaea began to break apart in the latest Triassic and earliest Jurassic, the monsoonal climate changed. The Western Interior of North America was slowly rotating into a position farther north of the equator. Soon, the Colorado Plateau was to become a Sahara.

Extensive eolian sand seas, called *ergs*, blew across the Colorado Plateau during the Lower Jurassic (figure 16). The region was located about 18° north latitude at the beginning of the Jurassic and about 30-35° north latitude at the end of the Jurassic (Kocurek and Dott, 1983; Peterson, 1994).

This is the latitude of the trade wind belt. Most modern hot deserts of the world occur within the trade wind belt and during the Jurassic, the climate of the Colorado Plateau appears similar to the modern Western Sahara.

The western edge of the continent was marked by a continental-margin magmatic arc, a product of subduction processes that began in the Triassic (Dubiel, 1994) and reached its maximum development in the Cretaceous. At the beginning of the Middle Jurassic Period, the western Elko highlands emerged to the west of the Utah-Idaho trough. The highlands record an irregular, pulsed orogeny (Peterson, 1994).

Middle Jurassic strata on the Colorado Plateau represent a complex interfingering of marine and nonmarine environments. The sediments were deposited during five major transgressive-regressive cycles (Peterson, 1994). A picture emerges of broad tidal flats marginal to a shallow sea that lay to the west (Wright *et al.*, 1962). The sea encroached into west-central Utah from the north and lay in the Utah-Idaho trough bordered to the west by the Elko Highlands.

As plate tectonic activity increased at the end of the Middle Jurassic and beginning of the Late Jurassic (about 157 Ma), a major transgression of the inland seaway forever destroyed the vast eolian sand seas that once covered the Colorado Plateau (Kocurek and Dott, 1983). Tidal flats covered the area as marine environments pushed south. The extensive Upper Jurassic, Morrison Formation was deposited across the continental Western United States (figure 17). Morrison depositional environments were quite varied. Sediments were deposited in mudflats, overbank floodplains, stream channels, small eolian sand fields, and scattered lakes and ponds (Peterson, 1994).

During the Jurassic, the subducting oceanic slab that was sliding eastward beneath the continental lithosphere probably changed its angle of descent and became steeper. This change caused the volcanic arc to develop farther to the west near the present-day border of California and Nevada. The late Jurassic and earliest Cretaceous magmatic activity associated with the volcanic arc is called the Nevadan orogeny. Volcanic ash was spread across the Colorado Plateau. The Nevadan Orogeny evolved into the late Cretaceous Sevier Orogeny as the rate of lithospheric plate movement increased.

The Sevier Orogeny formed a roughly north-south trending thrust belt that is well defined in present-day southern Nevada, central Utah, and western Montana (figure 18). A series of eastward-directed overthrusts carried upper Precambrian and lower Paleozoic sedimentary rocks over upper Paleozoic and lower Mesozoic rocks (Stewart, 1980). Today, the eastward limit of Sevier thrusting is exposed in the jagged peaks of the north-south trending Wasatch Range.

As the mountains rose in the west and the roughly north- south foreland trough expanded, the Gulf of Mexico separating North and South America continued to rift open in the south, and marine water began to spill into the basin. At the same time, marine water began to transgress from the Arctic region.

The sea advanced, retreated, and readvanced many times during the Cretaceous until the most extensive interior seaway ever to cover the continent drowned much of western North America. The Western Interior Seaway was an elongate basin that extended from today's Gulf of Mexico to the Arctic Ocean, a distance of about 4827 km (3,000 mi) (Kauffman, 1977). During periods of maximum transgression, the width of the basin was 1600 km (1,000 mi). The basin was relatively unrestricted at either terminus (Kauffman, 1977).

In the Four Corners region, the advances and retreats of the Cretaceous shoreline created a myriad of environments including incised river valley systems, estuaries, coal swamps, lagoons, delta systems, beaches, and offshore marine deposits. The interfingering of these environments is very complex, and the sedimentary rocks formed from the sediments include a variety of formations that have been grouped together into the *Dakota Formation* in western Colorado and eastern Utah (figure 22) and the *Dakota Group* in eastern Colorado.

The coarse conglomeratic sandstones, cross-stratification, petrified wood fragments, and erosional topography of the lower part of the Dakota Sandstone in the Hovenweep area suggests that the sediments were deposited by fluvial processes in paleovalleys incised into the underlying strata (Ekren and Houser, 1965; Condon, 1991; Elder and Kirkland, 1994).

At the beginning of Late Cretaceous time, the interior seaway had advanced to cover the eastern third of the Colorado Plateau. Gradually, as sea level rose, the soft, fissile, sparsely fossiliferous, dark- gray shale of the Mancos Shale was deposited in the deepening basin above the Dakota Sandstone.

Tertiary deposits are not exposed in the Hovenweep National Monument area, but a brief history of events affecting the Colorado Plateau region is described here for completeness. At the end of the Cretaceous, the tectonic plates were actively jockeying for position on the western margin of the continent. Plutons were being emplaced beneath the Sierra Nevada, and for the first time, granitic plutons were being emplaced in a southwest- northeast trend from southwestern Colorado to north- central Colorado (Christiansen *et al.*, 1994). The rearrangement of the tectonic plates gave rise to the Laramide Orogeny, the mountain- building episode that began the development of the modern Rocky Mountains.

The Laramide Orogeny began about 66 to 70 million years ago, in the late Cretaceous, and continued intermittently until about 35- 50 million years ago.

The Laramide event transformed the extensive basin of the Cretaceous Interior Seaway into smaller interior basins bordered by high arches (anticlines and synclines on the scale of miles). However, the Colorado Plateau region appears to have reacted as a single block to the crustal forces that buckled the rest of the central Rocky Mountains. The sedimentary strata on the Colorado Plateau was primarily warped into broad anticlinal and synclinal folds and great monoclines with very little brittle faulting (Dickinson and Snyder, 1978; Chapin and Cather, 1983; Hamilton, 1988; Erslev, 1993).

Then, from about 26- 35 Ma, in the Oligocene epoch, volcanic activity erupted across Utah. The laccoliths that formed the Henry Mountains, La Sal Mountains, and Abajo Mountains were emplaced during mid- Tertiary volcanism that gave rise to the extensive San Juan volcanic field in Colorado. A period of volcanic quiescence followed from about 16 to 19 Ma. During this time, the western United States underwent a radical tectonic transformation wherein the compressional regime that had existed for millions of years became an extensional regime. As the crust was extended, the surface was broken into the basin- and- range, block-faulted topography we see today in western Utah and Nevada.

Block faulting and volcanism, however, were secondary to the uplift of the Colorado Plateau that occurred between 5 and 10 Ma (Hintze, 1988). The entrenchment of the Colorado River and its tributaries occurred at this time. Tertiary sediments are missing from Hovenweep, but extensional faulting and basaltic volcanism in the western United States have continued into the present.

Two or three million years ago, early in the Quaternary, a broad uplift of the entire region initiated another period of active erosion. During the cooler, more humid climates of Pleistocene glaciation, streams cut headward into canyons, developing the drainage pattern seen today on the Colorado Plateau. Meltwater from glaciers brought more gravel deposits into the area. Wind from the southwest brought silt onto the Mesa Verde that developed into the rich, fertile soil exploited by the Anasazi.

During Pleistocene glaciation (1.6 Ma to 10,000 years ago), locally on the Colorado Plateau, glaciers formed at elevations below 1,828 m (6,000 ft) (Jim Johnson, Mesa State College, retired, personal communication, 2001). Definitive evidence of glaciation is difficult to find on the plateaus. Unlike glacial moraines contained in alpine valleys such as those along the Front Range, the moraines on the plateaus do not form distinct patterns. In the West Mancos region, west of Hovenweep National Monument in southwestern Colorado – southeastern Utah, glaciers flowing from the La Plata Mountains reached an elevation of at least 2,620 m (8,600 ft) above sea level, but the maximum extent is questionable (Jim Johnson, personal communication, 2001).

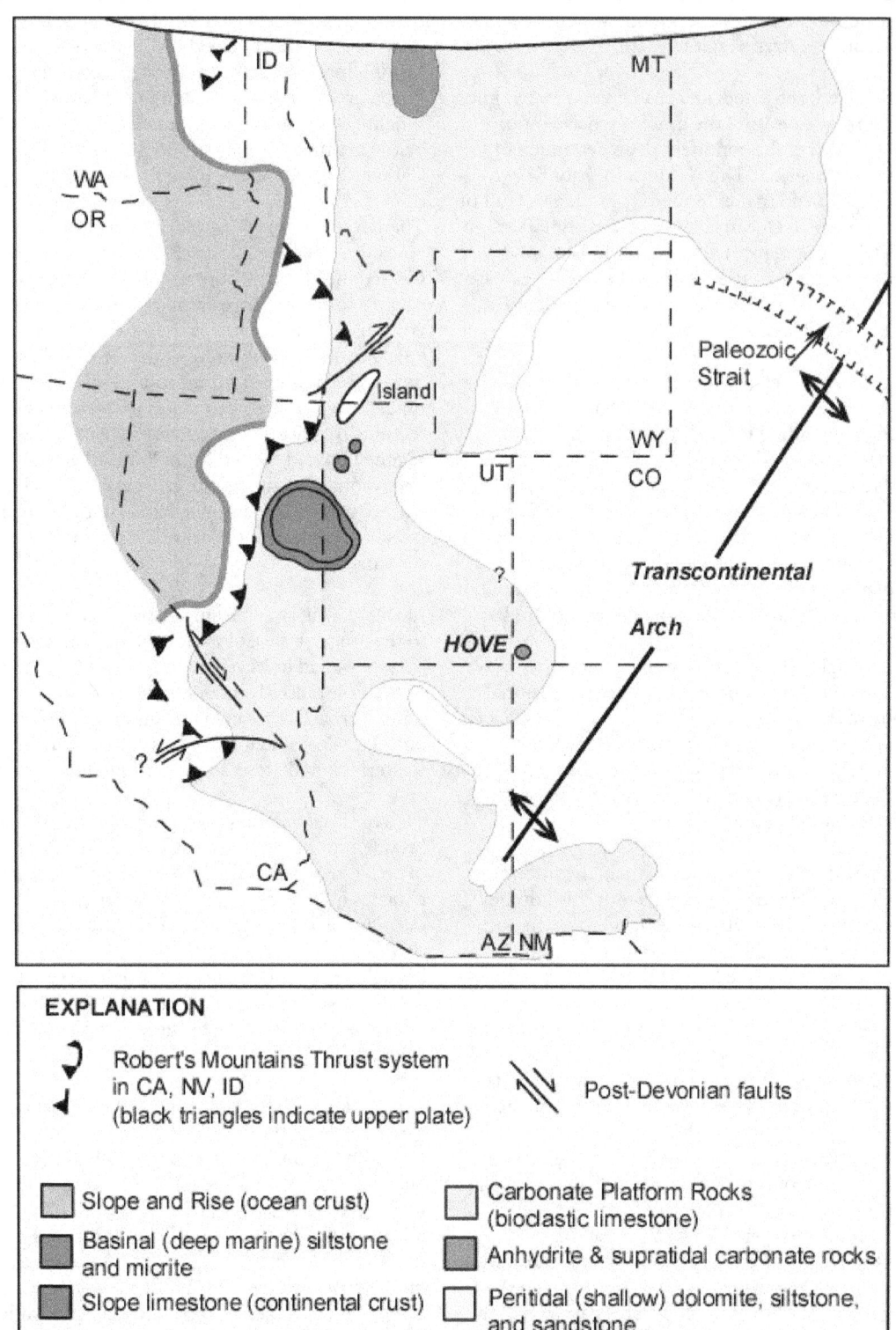

Figure 12: Distribution of lithofacies during the Upper Devonian, Frasnian stage of western United States. The red line is the strontium isotope line wherein $^{87}Sr/^{86}Sr = 0.706$ and is interpreted to represent the break between continental and oceanic crust. HOVE: Hovenweep National Monument. Modified from Johnson et al., 1991.

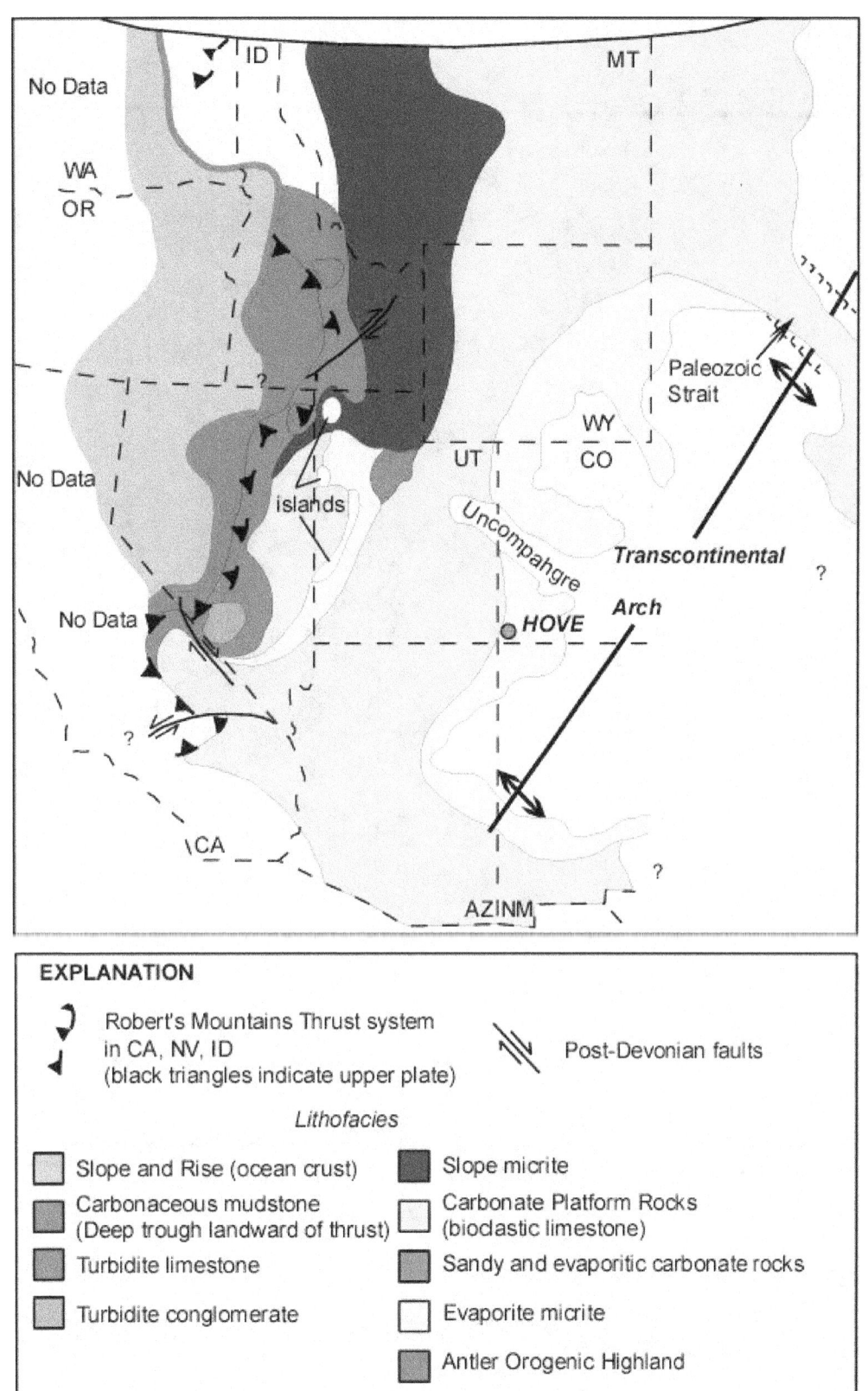

Figure 13: Lithofacies map of the Lower Mississippian Period, Kinderhookian stage of the western United States. While the lithofacies are complex in the foreland basin adjacent to the Antler orogenic highland, a broad carbonate platform developed to the east. Marine water breached the Transcontinental Arch through the Paleozoic Strait. HOVE: Hovenweep National Monument. Any Mississippian rocks that were deposited on the transcontinental Arch or ancestral Uncompahgre highland during this time have been eroded. Modified from Poole and Sandberg, 1991.

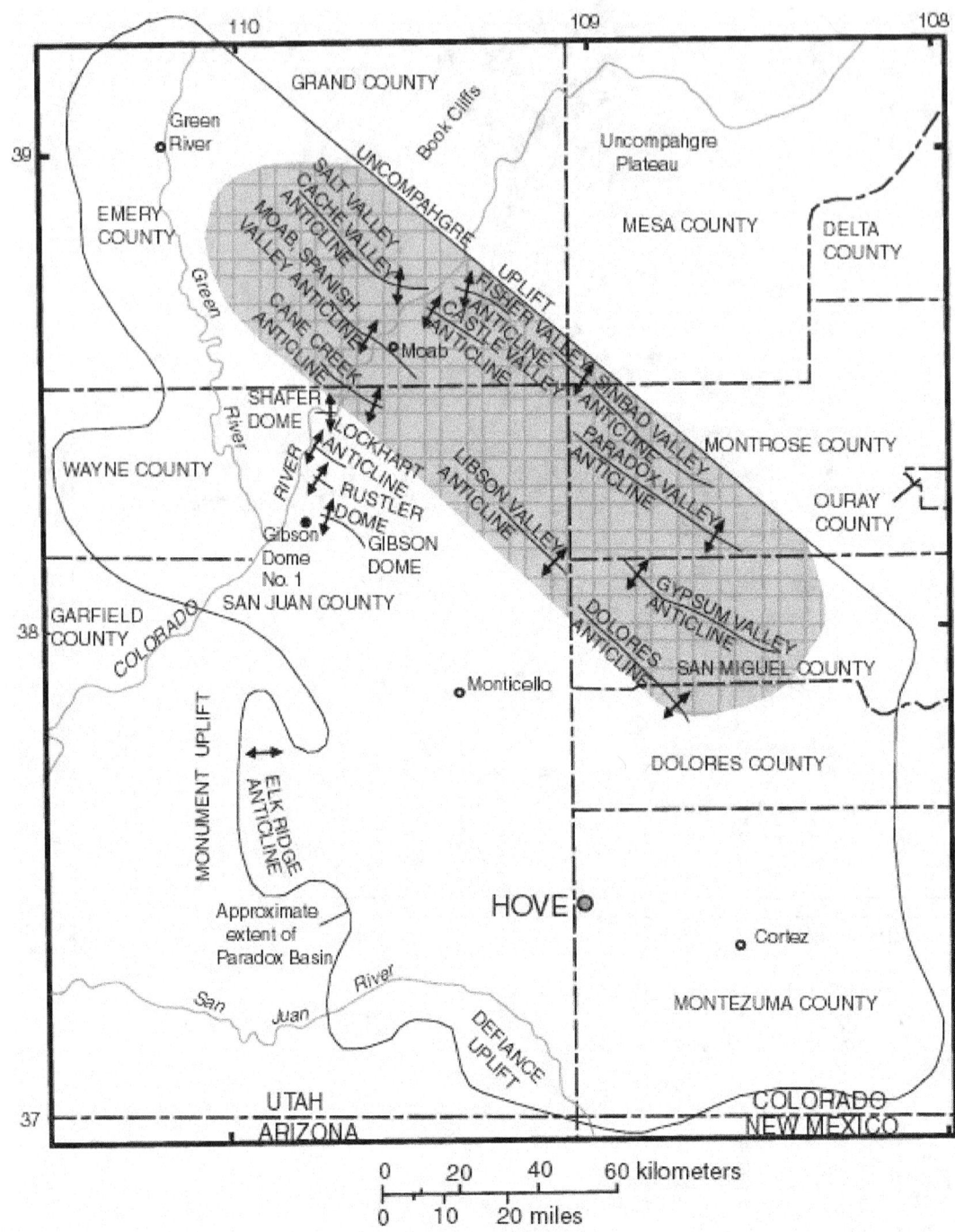

Figure 14: Map of the Paradox Basin. Heavy line represents the approximate limits of halite in the Middle Pennsylvanian Paradox Formation. Shaded area is the location of the Uncompahgre trough on the west-southwest border of the Uncompahgre uplift. HOVE: Hovenweep National Monument headquarters. Modified from Rueger (1996).

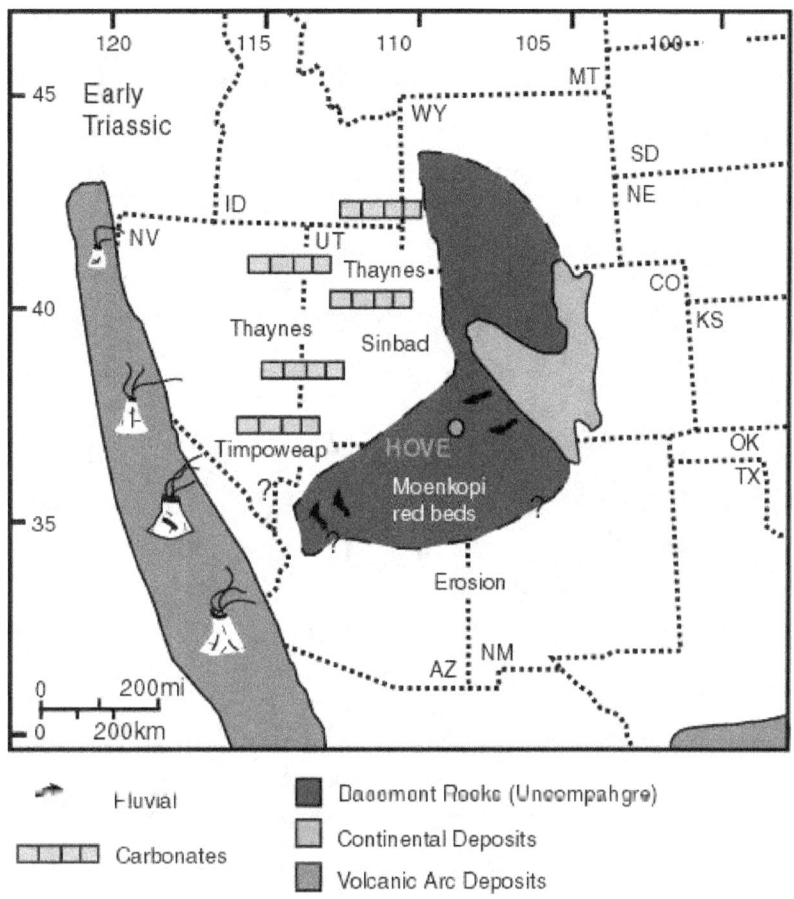

Figure 15: Paleogeographic map of the Lower Triassic, Moenkopi Formation during the second transgressive episode of the Early Triassic. HOVE: Hovenweep National Monument. Modified from Dubiel, 1994.

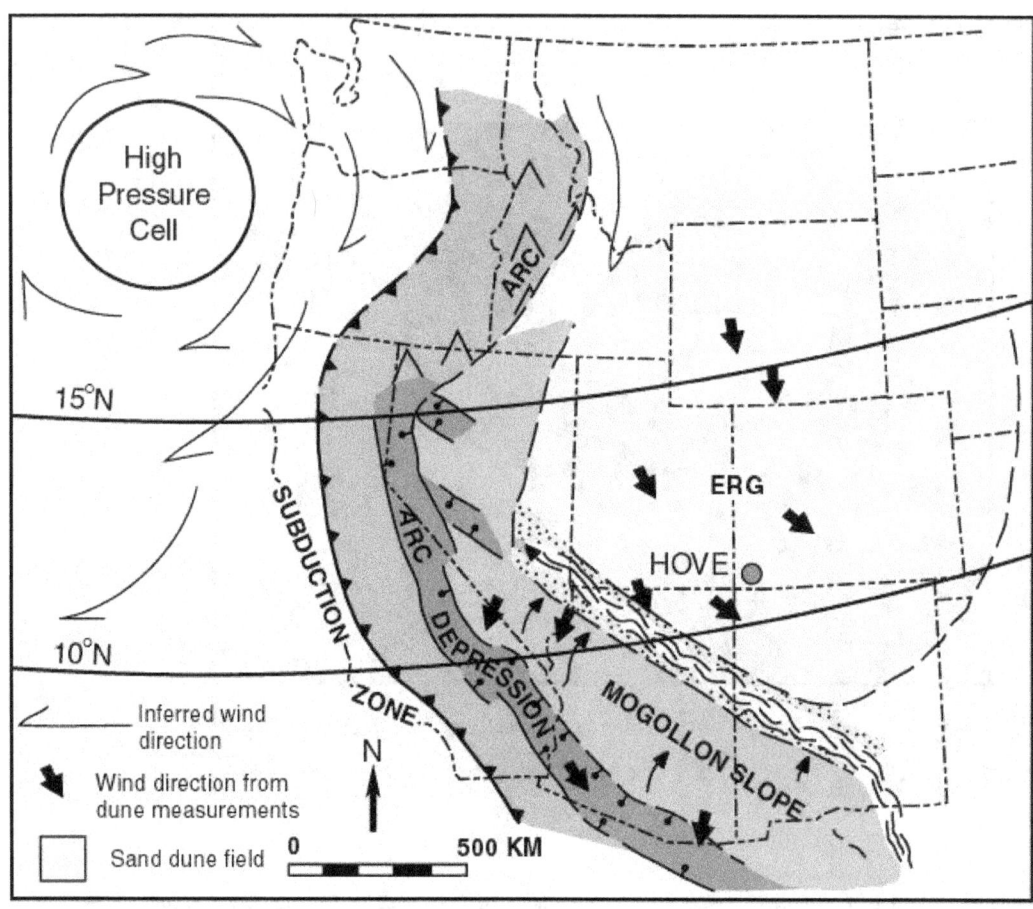

Figure 16: Paleogeographic map of the Lower Jurassic Period. Thick arrows indicate eolian transport of sand. Thin arrows indicate fluvial transport of sediments. Inverted "Vs" indicate the location of the volcanic arc. Solid triangles indicate the location of the subduction zone with the triangles on the overriding, upper lithospheric plate. HOVE: Hovenweep National Monument. Modified from Lawton (1994).

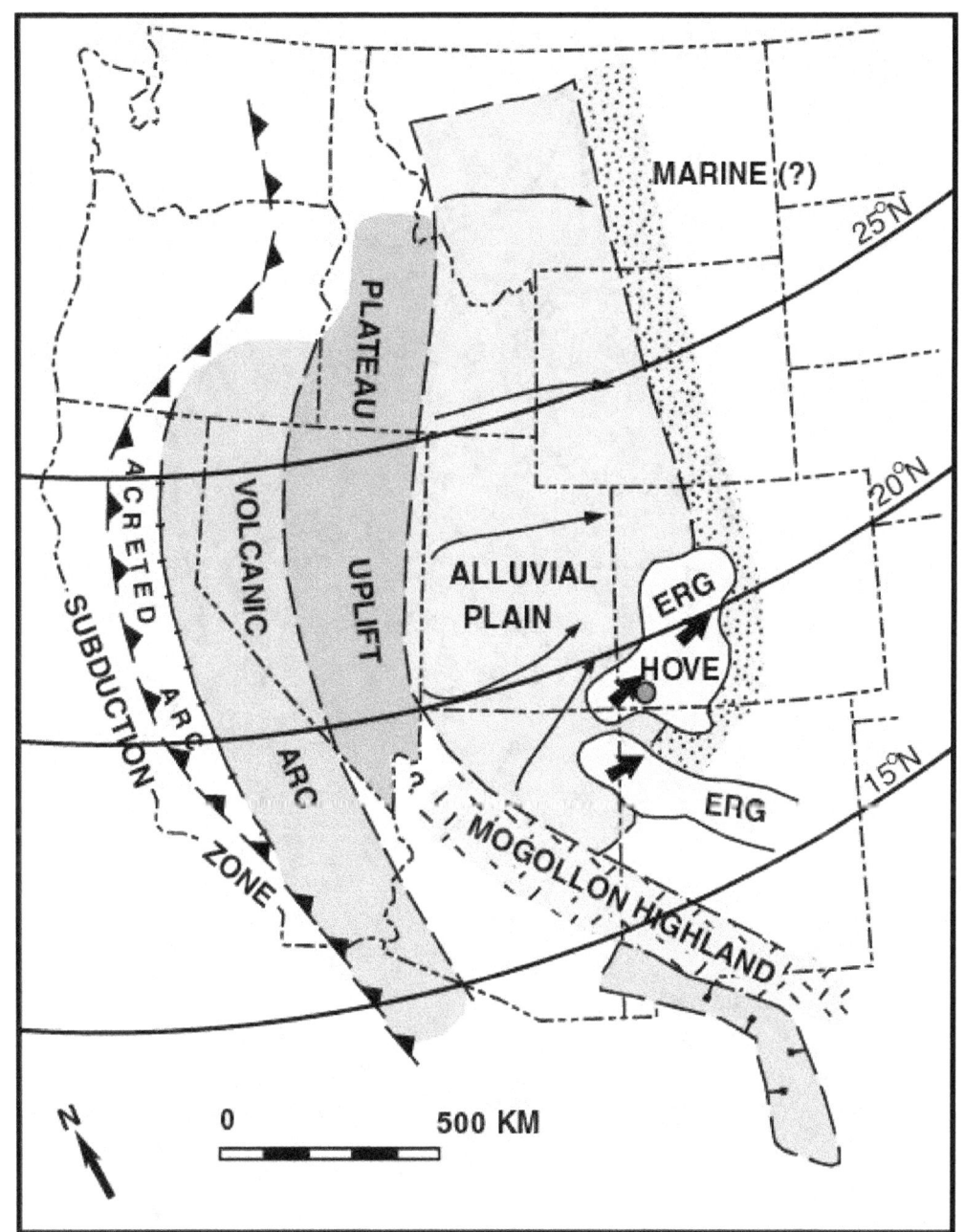

Figure 17: Upper Jurassic Period paleogeography. Thin arrows indicate fluvial dispersal. Thick arrows indicate wind directions. Sawteeth indicate the location of the subduction zone with the teeth on the overriding lithospheric plate. A marine environment possibly covered continental environments to the east. The alluvial plain expanded to the east with time. Modified from Lawton (1994).

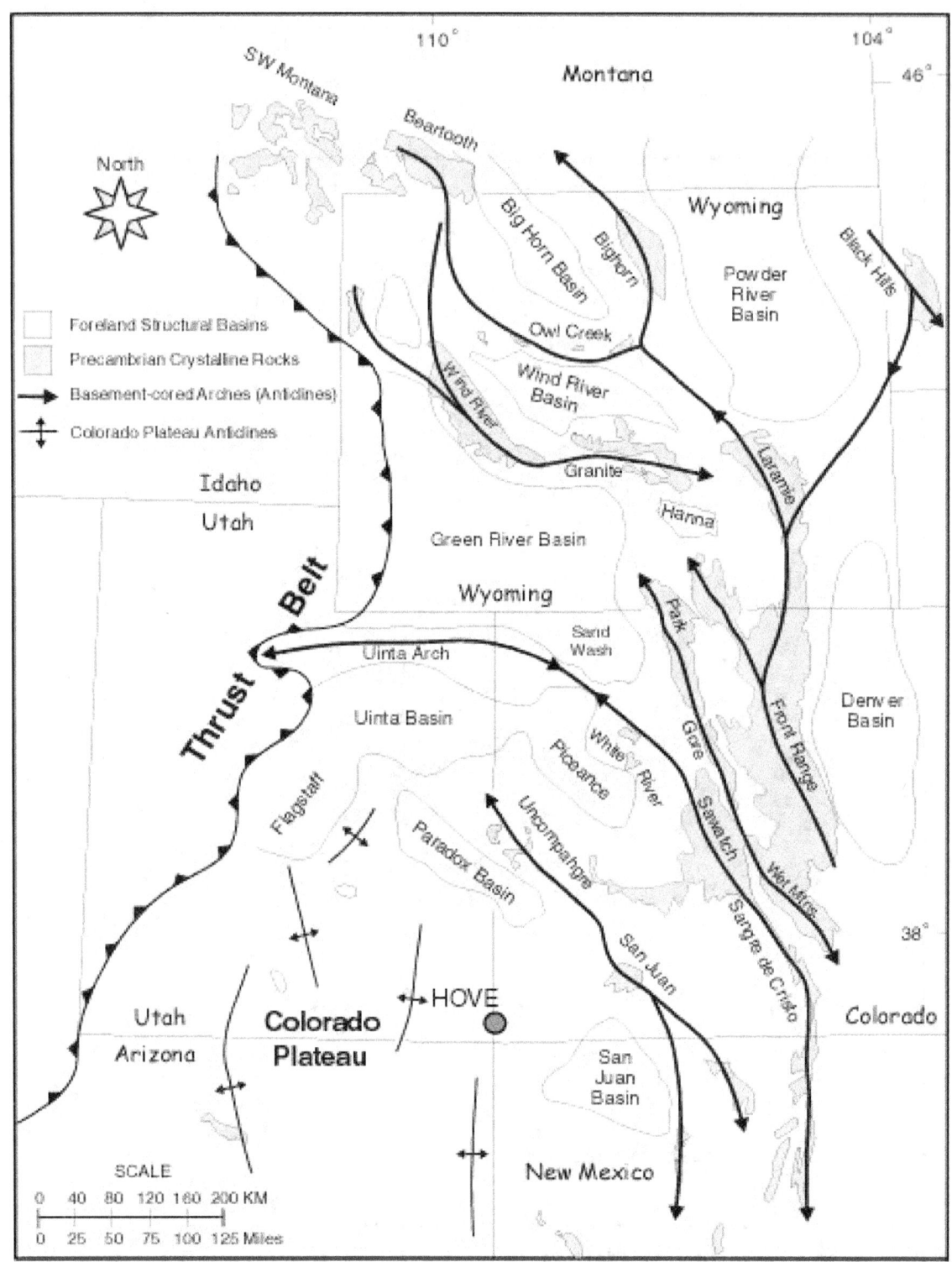

Figure 18: Location of Hovenweep National Monument (HOVE) on a tectonic map of the Laramide foreland. The map illustrates the anastamosing nature of the basement-cored arches (regional-scale anticlines) and the spatial relationships with the adjacent thrust belt, Colorado Plateau, and North American craton. From Gregson and Chure, 2000.

Eon	Era	Period	Epoch		Life Forms	N. American Tectonics
Phanerozoic (Phaneros = "evident", zoic = "life")	Cenozoic	Quaternary	Recent, or Holocene	Age of Mammals	Modern man	Cascade volcanoes
			Pleistocene		Extinction of large mammals and birds	Worldwide glaciation
			—1.6—			
		Tertiary	Pliocene		Large carnivores	Uplift of Sierra Nevada
			—5.3—		Whales and apes	Linking of N. & S. America
			Miocene			
			—23.7—			Basin-and-Range Extension
			Oligocene			
			—36.6—			
			Eocene		Early primates	Laramide orogeny ends (West)
			—57.8—			
			Palaeocene			
		—66.4—				
	Mesozoic	Cretaceous		Age of Dinosaurs	**Mass extinctions** Placental mammals Early flowering plants	Laramide orogeny (West) Sevier orogeny (West) Nevadan orogeny (West)
		—144—			First mammals	Elko orogeny (West)
		Jurassic			Flying reptiles	Breakup of Pangea begins
		—208—			First dinosaurs	Sonoma orogeny (West)
		Triassic				
	—245—					
	Paleozoic	Permian		Age of Amphibians	**Mass extinctions** Coal-forming forests diminish	Super continent Pangea intact Ouachita orogeny (South) Alleghenian (Appalachian) orogeny (East)
		—286—			Coal-forming swamps	Ancestral Rocky Mts. (West)
		Pennsylvanian			Sharks abundant Variety of insects	
		—320—			First amphibians	
		Mississippian			First reptiles	Antler orogeny (West)
		—360—			**Mass extinctions**	
		Devonian		Fishes	First forests (evergreens)	Acadian orogeny (East-NE)
		—408—				
		Silurian			First land plants	
		—438—			**Mass extinctions**	
		Ordovician		Marine Invertebrates	First primitive fish Trilobite maximum Rise of corals	Taconic orogeny (NE)
		—505—				
		Cambrian			Early shelled organisms	Avalonian orogeny (NE) Extensive oceans cover most of N. America
	—570—					
Proterozoic ("Early life")		Precambrian			1st multicelled organisms	Formation of early supercontinent
						First iron deposits
					Jellyfish fossil (670Ma)	Abundant carbonate rocks
Archean ("Ancient")			2500			
					Early bacteria & algae	
			~3800			Oldest known Earth rocks (~3.93 billion years ago)
Hadean ("Beneath the Earth")					Origin of life?	Oldest moon rocks (4-4.6 billion years ago)
						Earth's crust being formed
			4600		Formation of the Earth	

Figure 19: Geologic Time Scale. Red lines indicate major unconformities between eras. Included are major events in life history and tectonic events occurring North American continent. Absolute ages shown are in millions of years and are from the United States Geological Survey (USGS) time scale found at: http://geology.wr.usgs.gov/docs/usgsnps/gtime/timescale.html.

References

The following is a list of scientific literature references for the geologic resources evaluation of Hovenweep National Monument, many of the authors are cited in this report, others are included for general reference purposes.

Aubrey, William M., 1991, Geologic framework and stratigraphy of Cretaceous and Tertiary rocks of the southern Ute Indian Reservation, southwestern Colorado: USGS Professional Paper 1505- B, 24 p.

Baars, Donald L., 2000, The Colorado Plateau: University of New Mexico press, Albuquerque, NM, 254 p.

Baars, Donald L, 1995, Navajo Country: University of New Mexico press, Albuquerque, NM, 255 p.

Becker, Luann, Poreda, Robert J., Hunt, Andrew G., Bunch, Theodore E., and Rampino, Michael, 2001, Impact event at the Permian- Triassic boundary: Evidence from extraterrestrial noble gases in fullerenes, in Science, Feb. 23, p. 1530- 1533.

Beus, S. S., 1980, Late Devonian (Frasnian) paleogeography and paleoenvironments in northern Arizona, in Thomas D. Fouch and Esther R. Magathan, eds., Paleozoic Paleogeography of the West- Central United States: Rocky Mountain Section, SEPM (Society for Sedimentary Geology), p. 55- 70.

Blakey, R. C., 1994, Paleogeographic and tectonic controls on some Lower and Middle Jurassic erg deposits, Colorado Plateau, in Mario V. Caputo, James A. Peterson, and Karen J. Franczyk, eds., Mesozoic Systems of the Rocky Mountain Region, USA: Rocky Mountain Section, SEPM (Society for Sedimentary Geology), Denver, CO., p. 273- 298.

Busby- Spera, C.J., 1988, Speculative tectonic model for the early Mesozoic arc of the southwest Cordilleran United States: Geology, v. 16, no. 12, p. 1121- 1125.

Busby- Spera, C.J., 1990, Reply on "Speculative tectonic model for the early Mesozoic arc of the southwest Cordilleran United States": Geology, v. 18, no. 3, p. 285- 286.

Campbell, J.A., 1980, Lower Permian depositional systems and Wolfcampian paleogeography, Uncompahgre basin, eastern Utah and southwestern Colorado, in T.D. Fouch, E.R. Magathan, eds., Paleozoic Paleogeography of the West- Central United States: Society of Economic Paleontologists and Mineralogists (SEPM), Rocky Mountain Section, p. 327- 340.

Chapin, Charles, E. and Steven M. Cather, 1983, Eocene tectonics and sedimentation in the Colorado Plateau – Rocky Mountain area, in James Lowell, ed., Rocky Mountain Foreland Basins and Uplifts: Rocky Mountain Association of Geologists, Denver, CO., p. 33- 56.

Chernicoff, S. and Venkatakrishnan, R., 1995, *Geology*, Worth Publishers, 593 p.

Christiansen, Eric II, Kowallis, Bart J., and Barton, Mark D., 1994, Temporal and spatial distribution of volcanic ash in Mesozoic sedimentary rocks of the Western Interior: an alternative record of Mesozoic magmatism, in Mario V. Caputo, James A. Peterson, and Karen J. Franczyk, eds., Mesozoic Systems of the Rocky Mountain Region, USA: Rocky Mountain Section, SEPM (Society for Sedimentary Geology), Denver, CO., p. 73- 94.

Cole, R.D., Moore, G.E., Trevena, A.S., Armin, R.A., and Morton, M.P., 1996, Lithofacies definition in Cutler and Honaker Trail Formations, Northeastern Paradox Basin, by sedimentologic observations and spectral gamma- ray data, in A.C. Huffman, Jr., W.R. Lund, and L.H. Godwin, eds., Geology and Resources of the Paradox Basin: Utah Geological Association Guidebook 25, p. 169- 178.

Condon, Steven, M., 1991, Geologic and structure contour map of the Ute Mountain Ute Indian Reservation and adjacent areas, southwest Colorado and northwest New Mexico: USGS Map I- 2083, Scale: 1:100,000.

Condon, Steven M., 1989, Stratigraphic sections of the Middle Jurassic Wanakah Formation, Cow Springs Sandstone, and adjacent rocks from Bluff, Utah, to Lupton, Arizona: U.S.G.S. Oil and Gas Investigations OC- 131.

Condon, S.M., and Huffman, A.C., Jr., 1988, Revisions in nomenclature of the Middle Jurassic Wanakah Formation, northwestern New Mexico and northeastern Arizona: U.S.G.S. Bulletin 1633- A, p. 1- 12.

Dane, C.H., 1935, Geology of the Salt Valley anticline and adjacent areas, Grand County, Utah: U.S.G.S. Bulletin 863, 184 p.

De Voto, R. H., 1980A, Mississippian stratigraphy and history of Colorado, in Harry C. Kent and Karen W. Porter, eds., Colorado Geology: Rocky Mountain Association of Geologists, p. 57- 70.

De Voto, R. H., 1980B, Pennsylvanian stratigraphy and history of Colorado, *in* Harry C. Kent and Karen W. Porter, eds., Colorado Geology: Rocky Mountain Association of Geologists, p. 71- 102.

Dickinson, W. R., and Snyder, W.S., 1978, Plate tectonics of the Laramide Orogeny, *in* V. Matthews III, ed., Laramide folding associated with basement block faulting in the western United States: Geological Society of America, Memoir 151, p. 355- 366.

Doelling, Hellmut H., 2000, Geology of Arches National Park, Grand County, Utah, *in* D.A. Sprinkel, T.C. Chidsey, Jr., and P.B. Anderson, eds., Geology of Utah's Parks and Monuments: Utah Geological Association Publication 28, p. 11- 36.

Dott, R.J., Jr., Byers, C.W., Fielder, G.W., Stenzel, S.R., and Winfree, K.E., 1986, Aeolian to marine transition in Cambro- Ordovician cratonic sheet sandstones of the northern Mississippi Valley, U.S.A.: Sedimentology, v. 33, p. 345- 367.

Dubiel, R. F., 1994, Triassic deposystems, paleogeography, and paleoclimate of the Western Interior, *in* Mario V. Caputo, James A. Peterson, and Karen J. Franczyk, eds., Mesozoic Systems of the Rocky Mountain Region, USA: Rocky Mountain Section, SEPM (Society for Sedimentary Geology), Denver, CO., p. 133- 168.

Dubiel, R. F., Huntoon, J. E., Condon, S. M., and Stanesco, J. D., 1996, Permian deposystems, paleogeography, and paleoclimate of the Paradox Basin and vicinity, *in* Mark W. Longman and Mark D. Sonnenfeld, eds., Paleozoic Systems of the Rocky Mountain Region: Rocky Mountain Section, SEPM (Society for Sedimentary Geology), p. 427- 443.

Dunham, R.J., 1978, Classification of carbonate rocks according to depositional texture, *in* W.H. Ham, ed., Classification of Carbonate Rocks – A Symposium: American Association of American Geologists, Memoir 1, p. 108- 121.

Dutton, C. E., 1882, The physical geology of the Grand Canyon district, *in* United States Geological Survey, 2nd Annual Report: Department of the Interior, Washington, D.C., pp. 47- 166.

Ekren, E.B. and Houser, F.N., 1965, Geology and petrology of the Ute Mountains area, Colorado: U.S.G.S. Professional Paper 481, scale 1:48,000.

Ekren, E.B. and Houser, F.N., 1959a, Preliminary geologic map of the Moqui SW quadrangle, Montezuma County, Colorado: U.S.G.S., Mineral Investigations Field Studies Map MF- 216, scale 1:24,000.

Ekren, E.B. and Houser, F.N., 1959b, Preliminary geologic map of the Cortez SW quadrangle, Montezuma County, Colorado: U.S.G.S., Mineral Investigations Field Studies Map MF- 217, scale 1:24,000.

Elder, William P. and Kirkland, James I., 1994, Cretaceous paleogeography of the southern Western Interior Region, *in* Mario V. Caputo, James A. Peterson, and Karen J. Franczyk, eds., Mesozoic Systems of the Rocky Mountain Region, USA: Rocky Mountain Section, SEPM (Society for Sedimentary Geology), Denver, CO., p. 415- 440.

Erslev, E. A., 1993, Thrusts, back- thrusts, and detachment of Rocky Mountain foreland arches, *in* C. J. Schmidt, R. B. Chase, and E. A. Erslev, eds., Laramide Basement Deformation in the Rocky Mountain Foreland of the Western United States: Geological Society of America, Special Paper 280, p. 339- 358.

Fassett, James E., 1985, Early Tertiary paleogeography and paleotectonics of the San Juan Basin area, New Mexico and Colorado, *in* R.M. Flores and S.S. Kaplan, eds., Cenozoic Paleogeography of West- Central United States: Rocky Mountain Section, SEPM (Society for Sedimentary Geology), p. 317- 334.

Fewkes, J.W., 1919, Prehistoric villages, castles, and towers of southwestern Colorado: Bureau of American Ethnology, Smithsonian Institution, Bulletin 70, p. 44- 60.

Fillmore, R., 2000, The Geology of the Parks, Monuments and Wildlands of Southern Utah: The University of Utah Press, 268 p.

Folk, R.L., 1978, Spectral subdivision of limestone types, *in* W.H. Ham, ed., Classification of Carbonate Rocks – A Symposium: American Association of Petroleum Geologists, Memoir 1, p. 62- 84.

Gregson, J., 1992, Geology and tectonics of the Ancestral Uncompahgre Uplift and the Colorado Orogeny, *in* Joe D. Gregson, ed., Uncompahgria Journal: Mesa State Geology Department, Grand Junction, Colorado, p. 19- 46.

Gregson, Joe D. and Chure, Dan J., 2000, Geology and paleontology of Dinosaur National Monument, Utah- Colorado, *in* Douglas A. Sprinkel, Thomas C. Chidsey, Jr., and Paul B. Anderson, eds., Geology of Utah's Parks and Monuments: Utah Geological Association, Publication 28, p. 61- 83.

Griffitts, Mary O., 1990, Guide to the Geology of Mesa Verde National Park, Mesa Verde Museum Association, Inc., Mesa Verde National Park, CO., 88 p.

Griffitts, Mary O., 1994, Experiments with impregnation of Dakota Sandstone in Hovenweep National Monument, 1991- 1994: Unpublished National Park Service report, 49 p.

Hackman, R.J., 1955, Photogeologic Map of the Aneth- 1 Quadrangle San Juan County, Utah, and Montezuma County, Colorado: U.S.G.S. Map I- 90, Scale 1:24,000.

Hamilton, W. B., 1988, Laramide crustal shortening, *in* C.J. Schmidt and W.J. Perry, Jr., eds., Interaction of the Rocky Mountain foreland and the Cordilleran thrust belt: Geological Society of America, Memoir 171, p. 27- 39.

Hanson, W.R., 1975, The Geologic Story of the Uinta Mountains: U.S.G.S. Bulletin 1291, 144 p.

Harr, Clarence L., 1996, Paradox oil and gas potential of the Ute Mountain Ute Indian Reservation, *in* A.C. Huffman, Jr., W.R. Lund, and L.H. Godwin, eds., Geology and Resources of the Paradox Basin: Utah Geological Association Guidebook 25, 1996 Field Symposium, p. 13- 28.

Haynes, D. D., Vogel, J. D., and Wyant, D G., 1972, Geology, structure, and uranium deposits of the Cortez Quadrangle, Colorado and Utah: USGS Map I- 629, Scale 1:250,000.

Hintze, L.F., 1988, Geologic history of Utah: Brigham Young University Studies Special Publication 7, 202 p.

Hite, R.J., 1961, Potash- bearing evaporite cycles in the salt anticlines of the Paradox basin, Colorado and Utah: US.G.S. Professional Paper 424D, p. D136- D138.

Hite, R.J., 1970, Shelf carbonate sedimentation controlled by salinity in the Paradox Basin, southeast Utah, *in* J.L. Rau and L.F. Dellwig, eds., Third Symposium on Salt, v. 1: Northern Ohio Geological Society, p. 48- 66.

Hoffman, P.F., 1989, Precambrian geology and tectonic history of North America, *in* A.W. Bally and A.R. Palmer, eds., The Geology of North America; An Overview: Geological Society of America, The Geology of North America, v. A, p. 447- 512.

Huber, B. T., Norris, R. D., MacLeod, K. G., 2002, Deep-sea paleotemperature record of extreme warmth during the Cretaceous: Geological Society of America, Geology, v. 30, no. 2, p. 123- 126.

Huntoon, J. E., Stanesco, J. D., Dubiel, Russell F., and Dougan, J., 2000, Geology of Natural Bridges National Monument, Utah, *in* D.A. Sprinkel, T.C. Chidsey, Jr., and P.B. Anderson, eds., Geology of Utah's Parks and Monuments: Utah Geological Association Publication 28, p. 233- 250.

Hutchinson, R. M., 1976, Precambrian geochronology of western and central Colorado and southern Wyoming, *in* R. C. Epis and R. J. Weimer, eds., Studies in Colorado Field Geology: Professional Contributions, Colorado School of Mines, p. 73- 77.

Johnson, J.G., Klapper, G., and Sandberg, C.A., 1985, Devonian eustatic fluctuations in Euramerica: Geological Society of America Bulletin, v. 96, p. 567- 587.

Johnson, J.G., Sandberg, Charles A., and Poole, Forrest G., 1991, Devonian lithofacies of western United States, *in* John D. Cooper and Calvin H. Stevens, eds., Paleozoic Paleogeography of the Western United States – II: Society of Economic Paleontologists and Mineralogists (SEPM), Pacific Section, p. 83- 106.

Kauffman, E. G., 1977, Geological and biological overview: Western Interior Cretaceous Basin: Mountain Geologist, v. 14, p. 75- 99.

Kirkland, James I., Leckie, R. Mark, and Elder, William P., 1995, A new principal reference section for the Mancos Shale (Late Cretaceous) at Mesa Verde National Park, *in* Vincent L. Santucci and Lindsay McClelland, eds., National Park Service Paleontological Research: US Department of Interior, National Park Service Technical Report NPS/NRPO/NRTR- 95/16, Denver, CO., p. 77- 81.

Kocurek, G. and Dott, R. H. Jr., 1983, Jurassic paleogeography and paleoclimate of the central and southern Rocky Mountain region, *in* Mitchell W. Reynolds and Edward D. Dolly, eds., Mesozoic Paleogeography of the West- Central United States: Rocky Mountain Section, SEPM (Society for Sedimentary Geology), Denver, CO., p. 101- 118.

Lageson, D.R., and Spearing, D.R., 1988, Roadside Geology of Wyoming: Mountain Press Publishing Company, Missoula, 271 p.

Lawton, Timothy F., 1994, Tectonic setting of Mesozoic sedimentary basins, Rocky Mountain region, United States, *in* Mario V. Caputo, James A. Peterson, and Karen J. Franczyk, eds., Mesozoic Systems of the Rocky Mountain Region, USA: Rocky Mountain Section, SEPM (Society for Sedimentary Geology), Denver, CO., p. 1- 26.

Marzolf, J.E., 1990, Comment on "Speculative tectonic model for the early Mesozoic arc of the southwest Cordilleran United States": Geology, v. 18, no. 3, p. 285- 286.

Molenaar, C. M., 1983, Major depositional cycles and regional correlations of Upper Cretaceous rocks, southern Colorado Plateau and adjacent areas, *in* Mitchell W. Reynolds and Edward D. Dolly, eds., Mesozoic Paleogeography of the West- Central United States: Rocky Mountain Section, SEPM (Society for Sedimentary Geology), Denver, CO., p. 201- 224.

National Monument Service, 1990, Statement of Management: Hovenweep National Monument: Rocky Mountain Region, National Monument Service, US Department of the Interior, 25 p.

Nobel, David Grant, 1991, Ancient Ruins of the Southwest: Northland Publishing, 218 p.

O'Sullivan, R.B., 1980a, Stratigraphic sections of Middle Jurassic San Rafael Group and related rocks from the Green River to the Moab area in east- central Utah: U.S.G.S. Miscellaneous Field Studies Map MF- 1247.

O'Sullivan, R.B., 1980b, Stratigraphic sections of Middle Jurassic San Rafael Group from Wilson Arc to Bluff in southeastern Utah: U.S.G.S. Oil and Gas Investigations Chart OC- 102.

Paull, Rachel K., and Paull, Richard, A., 1994, Lower Triassic transgressive- regressive sequences in the Rocky Mountains, eastern Great Basin, and Colorado Plateau, USA, *in* Mario V. Caputo, James A. Peterson, and Karen J. Franczyk, eds., Mesozoic Systems of the Rocky Mountain Region, USA: Rocky Mountain Section, SEPM (Society for Sedimentary Geology), Denver, CO., p. 169- 180.

Peterson, Fred, 1994, Sand dunes, sabkhas, stream, and shallow seas: Jurassic paleogeography in the southern part of the Western Interior Basin, *in* Mario V. Caputo, James A. Peterson, and Karen J. Franczyk, eds., Mesozoic Systems of the Rocky Mountain Region, USA: Rocky Mountain Section, SEPM (Society for Sedimentary Geology), Denver, CO., p. 233- 272.

Peterson, James A., 1980, Permian paleogeography and sedimentary provinces, west central United States, *in* Thomas D. Fouch and Esther R. Magathan, eds., Paleozoic Paleogeography of the West- Central United States: Rocky Mountain Section, SEPM (Society for Sedimentary Geology), p. 271- 292.

Pipiringos, G.N., and O'Sullivan, R.B., 1978, Principal unconformities in Triassic and Jurassic rocks, western interior United States – a preliminary survey: U.S.G.S. Professional Paper 1035- A, 29 p.

Plummer, C. C., McGeary, D., and Carlson, D. H., 1996, *Physical Geology*: McGraw- Hill, 577 p.

Poole, F.G., and Sandberg, C.A., 1991, Mississippian paleogeography and conodonts biostratigraphy of the western United States, *in* John D. Cooper and Calvin H. Stevens, eds., Paleozoic Paleogeography of the Western United States: Pacific Section, Society of Economic Paleontologists and Mineralogists (SEPM), v. 2, p. 107- 136.

Poole, F.G., Stewart, John H., Palmer, A.R., Sandberg, C.A., Madrid, R.J., Ross, R.J., Jr., Hintze, L.F., Miller, M.M., and Wrucke, C.T., 1992, Latest Precambrian to latest Devonian time; Development of a continental margin, *in* B.C. Burchfiel, P.W. Lipman, and M.L. Zoback, eds., The Cordilleran Orogen: Conterminous U.S.: Geological Society of America, The Geology of North America, v. G- 3, p. 9- 56.

Raup, D. M., 1991, Extinction: Bad Genes or Bad Luck?: W.W. Norton and Company, New York, 210 p.

Reed, J. C., Jr., Bickford, M. E., Premo, W. R., Aleinikoff, J. N., and Pallister, J. S., 1987, Evolution of the Early Proterozoic Colorado province: Constraints from U- Pb geochronology: Geology, v. 15, p. 861- 865.

Rice, D. D. and Shurr, G. W., 1983, Patterns of sedimentation and paleogeography across the Western Interior Seaway during time of deposition of Upper Cretaceous Eagle Sandstone and equivalent rocks, northern Great Plains, *in* Mitchell W. Reynolds and Edward D. Dolly, eds., Mesozoic Paleogeography of the West- Central United States: Rocky Mountain Section, SEPM (Society for Sedimentary Geology), p. 337- 358.

Rigby, J. K., 1977, Southern Colorado Plateau: Kendall/Hunt Publishing Company, Dubuque, IA., 148 p.

Ross, R. J. and Tweto, O., 1980, Lower Paleozoic sediments and tectonics in Colorado, *in* Harry C. Kent and Karen W. Porter, eds., Colorado Geology: Rocky Mountain Association of Geologists, p. 47- 56.

Rueger, Bruce F., 1996, Palynology and its relationship to climatically induced depositional cycles in the Middle Pennsylvanian (Desmoinesian) Paradox Formation of Southeastern Utah: U.S.G.S. Bulletin 2000- K, 4 plates, 22 p.

Sageman, Bradley B. and Arthur, Michael A., 1994, Early Turonian paleogeographic/paleobathymetric map, Western Interior, U.S., *in* Mario V. Caputo, James A. Peterson, and Karen J. Franczyk, eds., Mesozoic Systems of the Rocky Mountain Region, USA: Rocky Mountain Section, SEPM (Society for Sedimentary Geology), Denver, CO., p. 457- 470.

Santucci, Vincent L., 2000, A survey of the Paleontological Resources from the National Parks and Monuments in Utah, *in* D.A. Sprinkel, T.C. Chidsey, Jr., and P.B. Anderson, eds., Geology of Utah's Parks and Monuments: Utah Geological Association, Publication 28, p. 535- 556.

Scott, R. B., Harding, A. E., Hood, W. C., Cole, R. D., Livaccari, R. F., Johnson, J. B., Shroba, R. R., Dickerson, R. P., 2001, Geologic map of Colorado National Monument and adjacent areas, Mesa County, Colorado: U.S. Geological Survey, Geologic Investigations Series I- 2740, 1:24,000 scale.

Silberling, N. J. and Roberts, R. J., 1962, Pre- Tertiary stratigraphy and structure of northwestern Nevada: GSA Special Paper 72, 58 p.

Sloss, L.L., 1963, Sequences in the cratonic interior of North America: Geological Society of America Bulletin, v. 74, p. 93- 114.

Sloss, L.L., 1988, Tectonic evolution of the craton in Phanerozoic time, *in* L.L. Sloss, ed., Sedimentary Cover – North American Craton: U.S.: Geological Society of America, Geology of North America, Vol. D- 2, p. 25- 52.

Speed, R.C., 1983, Evolution of the sialic margin in the central western United States, *in* J.S. Watkins and C.L. Drake, eds., Studies in continental margin geology: American Association of Petroleum Geologists Memoir 34, p. 457- 468.

Stewart, J. H., 1980, Geology of Nevada: Nevada Bureau of Mines and Geology, Special Publication 4, 136 p.

Stewart, J.H., Poole, F.G., and Wilson, R.F., 1972A, Stratigraphy and Origin of the Triassic Moenkopi Formation and related Triassic strata in the Colorado Plateau region: U.S.G.S. Professional Paper 691, 195 p.

Stewart, J.H., Poole, F.G., and Wilson, R.F., 1972B, Stratigraphy and Origin of the Chinle Formation and related Triassic strata in the Colorado Plateau region: U.S.G.S. Professional Paper 690, 336 p.

Stone, D. S., 1986, Seismic and borehole evidence for important pre- Laramide faulting along the axial arch in northwest Colorado, *in* Donald S. Stone, ed., New Interpretations of Northwest Colorado Geology: Rocky Mountain Association of Geologists, p. 19- 36.

Tarbuck, E. J., Lutgens, F. K., and Dennis, T., 2001, *Earth: An Introduction to Physical Geology*: Prentice- Hall, 7th edition, 688 p.

Tonnsen, J. J., 1986, Influence of tectonic terranes adjacent to the Precambrian Wyoming province on Phanerozoic stratigraphy, *in* J. A. Peterson, ed., Paleotectonics and Sedimentation in the Rocky Mountain Region: American Association of Petroleum Geologists Memoir 41, p. 21- 39.

Tweto, O., 1980, Precambrian geology of Colorado, *in* Harry C. Kent and Karen W. Porter, eds., Colorado Geology: Rocky Mountain Association of Geologists, p. 37- 46.

Walker, Roger G., 1992, Facies, facies models and modern stratigraphic concepts, *in* Facies Models: Response to Sea Level Change: Roger G. Walker and Noel P. James, eds., Geological Association of Canada, p. 1- 14.

Warner, L.A., 1980, The Colorado Lineament, *in* H.C. Kent and K.W. Porter, eds., Colorado Geology: Rocky Mountain Association of Geologists, Denver, p. 11- 22.

Wanek, Alexander A., 1959, Geology and fuel resources of the Mesa Verde area Montezuma and La Plata Counties, Colorado: USGS Bulletin 1072- M, p. 667- 721.

Weimer, R.J., 1980, Recurrent movement on basement faults, a tectonic style for Colorado and adjacent areas, *in* Harry C. Kent and Karen W. Porter, eds., Colorado Geology: Rocky Mountain Association of Geologists, p. 23- 36.

Witzke, B. J., 1980, "Middle and Upper Ordovician paleogeography of the region bordering the Transcontinental Arch", *in* Thomas D. Fouch and Esther R. Magathan, eds., Paleozoic Paleogeography of the West- Central United States: Rocky Mountain Section, SEPM (Society for Sedimentary Geology), p. 1- 18.

Woodward, L.A., 1988, Tectonic map of the Rocky Mountain region of the United States, *in* Sloss, L.L., ed., Sedimentary Cover – North American Craton, U.S.: Geological Society of America, The Geology of North America Volume D- 2, Plate 2.

Wright, J.C., Shawe, D.R., and Lohman, S.W., 1962, Definition of members of Jurassic Entrada Sandstone in east- central Utah and west- central Colorado: American Association of Petroleum Geologists Bulletin, v. 46, no. 11, p. 2057- 2070.

Appendix A: Geologic Map Graphic

This image provides a preview or "snapshot" of the digital geologic map for Hovenweep National Monument which can be found on the included CD.

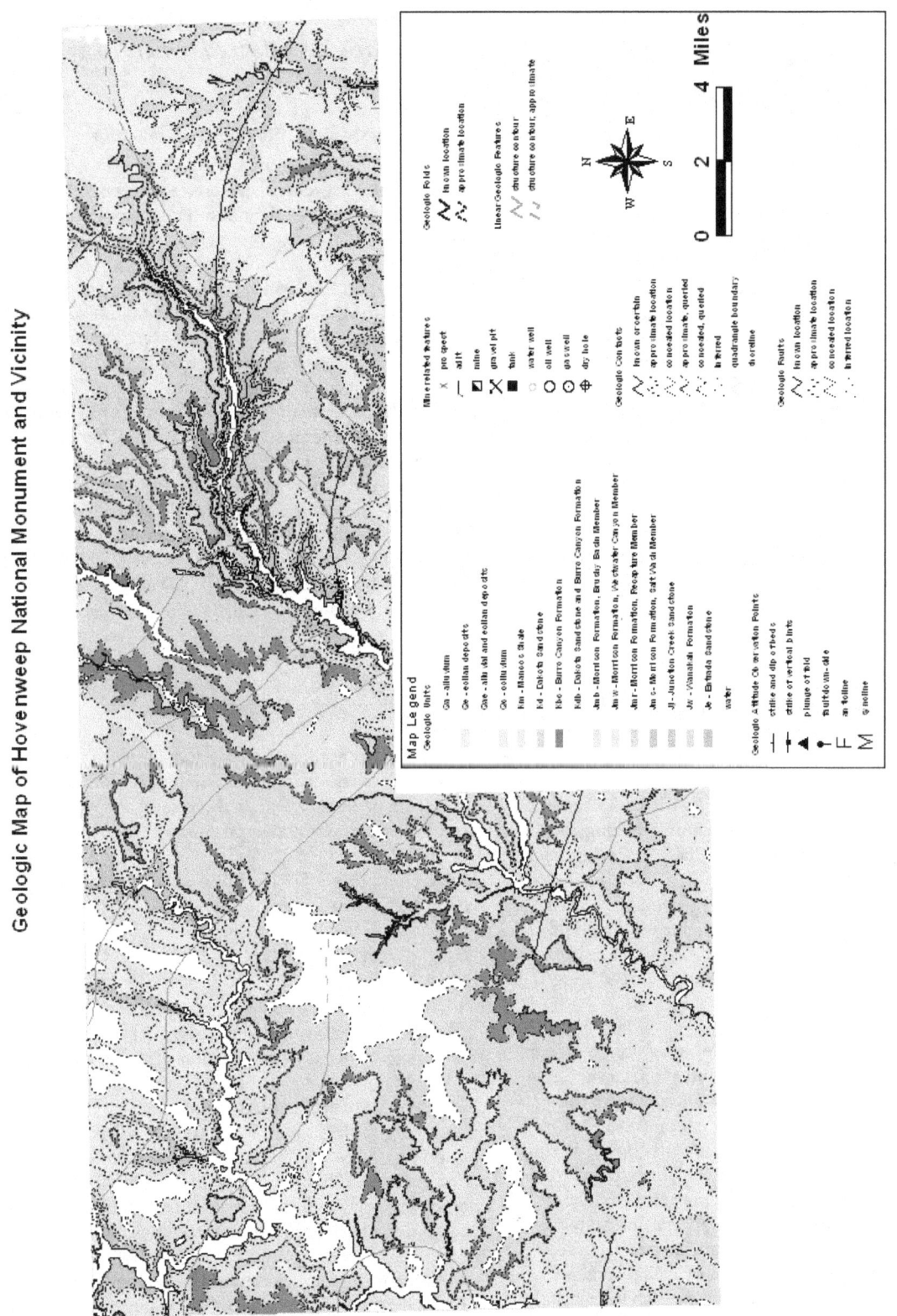

The original map digitized by NPS staff to create this product was: Poole, A., 2000, Geologic map of Hovenweep National Monument and the Surrounding Area, Colorado, NPS, unpublished, 1:24000 scale. For a detailed digital geologic map and cross sections, see included CD.

Appendix B: Southeast Utah Group Scoping Summary

The following excerpts are from the GRE Workshop Summary for the NPS Southeast Utah Group (SEUG) and provide regional geologic information. Although included in this group, a separate scoping meeting was held for Hovenweep National Monument September 5- 6, 2000. This summary is included as Appendix C. Both are historical documents and as such contact information and web addresses referred to herein may be outdated.

Executive Summary

An inventory workshop was held for national park service units in the Southeast Utah Group (Arches NP, Canyonlands NP, Hovenweep NM, and Natural Bridges NM) from May 24- 27, 1999 to view and discuss the geologic resources, to address the status of geologic mapping by the Utah Geological Survey (UGS) for compiling both paper and digital maps, and to assess resource management issues and needs. Cooperators from the NPS Geologic Resources Division (GRD), Natural Resources Information Division (NRID), Southeast Utah Group NPS staff (interpretation, natural resources, deputy superintendents), UGS, United States Geological Survey (USGS), and Utah Geological Association (UGA) were present for the two day workshop.

Monday May 24th involved a field trip to Natural Bridges NM (NABR) led by Red Rocks College geologist Jack Stanesco with additions from Christine Turner and Pete Peterson (both of the USGS).

Tuesday May 25th involved a field trip to Canyonlands NP (CANY) led by USGS geologist George Billingsley, again with additions from Christine Turner and Pete Peterson also of the USGS.

Wednesday May 26th involved a field trip to Arches NP (ARCH) led by UGS geologist Hellmut Doelling with additions from Grant Willis (UGS) and Vince Santucci (NPS- GRD).

An on- line slide show of the highlights of these field trips can be found at http://www.nature.nps.gov/grd/geology/gri/ut/seug/field_trip_seug

Thursday May 27th involved a scoping session to present overviews of the NPS Inventory and Monitoring (I&M) program, the Geologic Resources Division, and the ongoing Geologic Resources Evaluation (GRE) for Colorado and Utah. Round table discussions involving geologic issues for the Southeast Utah Group included interpretation, the UGA Millennium 2000 guidebook featuring the geology of Utah's National and State parks, paleontological resources, the status of cooperative geologic mapping efforts, sources of available data, geologic hazards, potential future research topics, and action items generated from this meeting. Brief summaries of each follows.

Overview of Geologic Resources Evaluation

After introductions by the participants, Joe Gregson (NPS- NRID) presented an overview of the NPS I&M Program, the status of the natural resource inventories, and the geological resources inventory.

He also presented a demonstration of some of the main features of the digital geologic map for the Black Canyon of the Gunnison NM and Curecanti NRA areas in Colorado. This has become the prototype for the NPS digital geologic map model as it ideally reproduces all aspects of a paper map (i.e. it incorporates the map notes, cross sections, legend etc.) with the added benefit of being a GIS component. It is displayed in ESRI ArcView shape files and features a built- in help file system to identify the map units. It can also display scanned JPG or GIF images of the geologic cross sections supplied with the map. The cross section lines (ex. A- A') are subsequently digitized as a shape file and are hyperlinked to the scanned images.

For a recap on this process, go to: http://www.nature.nps.gov/grd/geology/gri/blca_cure/ and view the various files in the directory.

The geologists at the workshop familiar with GIS methods were quite impressed with this method of displaying geologic maps digitally; Gregson is to be commended for his accomplishments.

Bruce Heise (NPS- GRD) followed with an introduction to the NPS GRD group.

Interpretation

The GRE also aims to help promote geologic resource interpretation within the parks and GRD has staff and technology to assist in preparation of useful materials including developing site bulletins and resource management proposal (RMP) statements appropriate to promoting geology. Jim Wood (GRD) and Melanie Moreno (USGS- Menlo Park, CA) have worked with several other NPS units in developing web- based geology interpretation themes, and should be considered as a source of assistance should the park desire.

Along the lines of interpretation of geology for the SEUG, it was suggested that they consider hiring a full- time geologist to be on staff to evaluate research proposals and generally assist all interpretive areas within the SEUG to find out what issues should be addressed. A geologist could add greatly to NABR, CANY, and ARCH because the primary theme of these parks is geologic; there would be no bridges, arches, or canyon (lands) without the underlying influence of geology and geologic processes upon this part of the world. A geologist would also certainly be active in establishing the most effective wayside exhibits aimed at informing the public about the geologic wonders of the area. A geologist can certainly assist in the presentation and interpretation of paleontologic resources and issues also.

Such a position could act as a liaison among various tour groups, researchers, field camps and professional organizations that visit the area because of the spectacular geology. Geologic hazards would also be able to be more fully understood. Obviously, effective communication skills are a highly desirable quality for any applicant.
In the absence of such a position, the GRD is most willing to assist the SEUG in any geologic matters and issues should they desire. Please contact Bruce Heise or Tim Connors to discuss further matters regarding geologic resources.

UGA Guidebook on Utah's National and State Park Areas

Doug Sprinkel of the UGA announced that a guidebook treating the geology of 27 of Utah's national and state parks and monuments will be compiled for publication in September 2000. This compilation will be a snapshot into the geology of each park and covers most facets of what the GRE is trying to develop for each park for a final report (i.e. cross sections, simplified geologic map, general discussions of rocks, structure, unique aspects of park geology, classic viewing localities). Each author will be encouraged to get with NPS staff interpreters to develop a product that aims at a wide audience (the common visitor, the technical audience and the teaching community). Authors for SEUG parks are as follows:
Arches NP: Hellmut Doelling (UGS)
Canyonlands NP: Donald Baars
Natural Bridges NM: Jackie Huntoon, Russell Dubiel, Jack Stanesco

Also, a CD-ROM will be distributed with the publication featuring road and trail logs for specific parks as well as a photo glossary and gallery. Park authors are strongly encouraged to get with NPS staff to make sure that any trail logs do follow maintained trails and do not take visitors into unauthorized areas, or places where resources are fragile and would be disturbed by increased visitation (i.e. areas with cryptogamic soils).

The photo glossary will describe certain geologic features (i.e. what is crossbedding?). These will also be available as web-downloadable Adobe Acrobat PDF files.

The UGA cannot copyright this material because it is funded with state money, so it can be distributed widely and freely, which will also benefit the purposes of the GRE. Additional reprints are not a problem because of the digital nature of the publication and the UGA board is committed to additional printings as needed. UGA normally prints 1000 copies of their publications because they become dated after about five years; that will probably not be an issue for this publication. Prices for the full-color guidebook are estimated to be approximately $25/copy, and sales are expected to be high (exact estimates for Capitol Reef NM were 125 copies/year). A website for the guidebook is forthcoming in October 1999.

Field Trips will be held in September 2000. Currently, four field trips are scheduled:
Arches NP, Canyonlands NP, Dead Horse Point State Park (SP)
Antelope Island SP and Wasatch Mountain SP
Southeast Utah Group NP, Cedar Breaks NM, Snow Canyon SP and Quail Creek SP
Dinosaur NM, Flaming Gorge NRA, and Red Fleet SP

Note: Trips 1 and 2 will run concurrently and Trips 3 and 4 will also run concurrently.

Many other benefits are anticipated from this publication and are enumerated below:
This type of project could serve as a model for other states to follow to bolster tourism and book sales promoting their state and its geologic features.

Sandy Eldredge (UGS) will be targeting teaching communities for involvement in the field trips; hopefully teachers will pass on what they have learned to their young audience.

The language is intended to appeal to someone with a moderate background in geology and yet will be very informative to the educated geologist.

The publication may be able to serve as a textbook to colleges teaching Geology of National Parks (in Utah).

A welcomed by-product could be roadlogs between parks in Utah for those visiting multiple parks, perhaps with a regional synthesis summarizing how the overall picture of Utah geology has developed.

Disturbed Lands

GRD's John Burghardt has done work in Lathrop Canyon on reclaiming abandoned mineral lands (aml). His reports should be studied as a significant source of data for this area to determine if additional work needs to be performed. Dave Steensen (GRD) heads the AML program and can also be contacted.

Paleontological Resources

The field trip at Arches NP provided glimpses into the paleontological resources (dinosaur bones) near Delicate

Arch. It has been suggested to keep this location low profile to minimize disturbances and potential theft or vandalism.

During the scoping session, the importance of a paleontological resource inventory for the Cedar Mountain and Morrison Formations near the Dalton Wells Quarry was discussed as being a priority. The important resources are likely to be dinosaur bones. A staff geologist or paleontologist would surely be useful for this purpose

Vince Santucci (NPS- GRD Paleontologist) will be co-authoring a "Paleontological Survey of Arches National Park" and detailing findings of resources within the park. Plants, invertebrates, and vertebrate tracksites are among the recognized paleontological resources within the Southeast Utah Group area parks.

Similar surveys have been done for Yellowstone and Death Valley NPs and have shed valuable new information on previously unrecognized resources. These surveys involve a literature review/bibliography and recognition of type specimens, species lists, and maps (which are unpublished to protect locality information), and also make park specific recommendations for protecting and preserving the resources.

The Death Valley Survey will be available soon. The Yellowstone Survey is already available on- line at:

http://www.nature.nps.gov/grd/geology/paleo/yell_survey/index.htm

and is also available as a downloadable PDF at http://www.nature.nps.gov/grd/geology/paleo/yell.pdf

Paleontological resource management plans should be produced for Southeast Utah Group involving some inventory and monitoring to identify human and natural threats to these resources. Perhaps someone on the park staff could be assigned to coordinate paleontological resource management and incorporate any findings or suggestions into the parks general management plan (GMP). It would be useful to train park staff (including interpreters and law enforcement) in resource protection, as the fossil trade "black market" has become quite lucrative for sellers and often results in illegal collecting from federal lands.

Collections taken from this area that now reside in outside repositories should be tracked down for inventory purposes. Fossils offer many interpretive themes and combine a geology/biology link and should be utilized as much as possible in interpretive programs.

Status of Geologic Mapping Efforts for the SEUG

Status of Existing Maps
It should be noted that the following paper geologic maps exist:

Arches NP ("Geologic Map of Arches National Park and vicinity, Grand County, Utah" by Hellmut H. Doelling, 1985) at 1:50,000. The area was mapped at 1:24,000 scale, but compiled at 1:50,000 scale.

Canyonlands NP ("Geologic Map of Canyonlands National Park and Vicinity, Utah" by George Billingsley, Peter Huntoon, and William J. Breed, 1982) at 1:62,500

Canyonlands NP ("Bedrock Geologic Map of Upheaval Dome, Canyonlands NP, Utah" by Gene Shoemaker, Herkenhoff and Kriens, 1997); scale unknown.

George Billingsley noted that when he worked on the Canyonlands map, he mostly compiled previous material. He thought several additions to the Quaternary deposits and the placement of joints/fractures on the maps would improve the quality of the 1982 Canyonlands map. There are also some issues regarding assignment of the Page Sandstone, and the controversy of the Dewey Bridge Member of the Entrada versus the Carmel Formation being within the map area. He thinks eventually, the entire area should be compiled at 1:24,000 to better enhance features and add to resource management.

Jackie Huntoon has told Bruce Heise that she is working on a digital coverage for Natural Bridges, but needs the hypsography (contour lines) to complete her work. Desired quadrangles that NRID has this coverage for are the following:
The Cheesebox
Woodenshoe Buttes
Kane Gulch
It is not sure if the coverage exists for the Moss Back Butte quadrangle; Joe Gregson will look into it.

Digitized Maps
The 1985 Arches map has been digitized into an ArcInfo coverage by SEUG staff. The attribute quality is unknown however, and will be researched. NPS- GRE folks will work with SEUG GIS Specialist Gery Wakefield to learn more about this coverage

The 1982 Canyonlands map is not known to have been digitized at this point and hopefully can be done by the SEUG GIS staff. George Billingsley says that the Canyonlands Natural History Association has the original line work and mylars; Diane Allen said she will contact them to see if they still have this work.

The 1997 Upheaval Dome map is digitized as an ArcInfo coverage and a copy was given to Craig Hauke (CANY) from George Billingsley. It also contains cross sections and a report. A website exists for this work at: http://www.seismo.unr.edu/ftp/pub/louie/dome/98seismo/index.html.
UGS Mapping Activities in SEUG area
Currently, the UGS is mapping in Utah at three different scales:

1:24,000 for high priority areas (i.e. National and State parks)
1:100,000 for the rest of the state
1:500,000 for a compiled state geologic map

The UGS plans to complete mapping for the entire state of Utah within 10- 15 years at 1:100,000 scale. For 1:100,000 scale maps, their goal is to produce both paper and digital maps; for 1:24,000 scale maps, the only digital products will be from "special interest" areas (i.e. areas such as Southeast Utah Group and growing metropolitan St. George). Grant Willis mentioned that the UGS simply does not have enough manpower and resources to do more areas at this scale. He also reiterated that UGS mapping goals are coincident with those of the National Geologic Mapping Program.

Grant Willis talked about the status of UGS mapping activities within the Southeast Utah Group area (see Appendix C for reviewing specific index maps for each park).

30 x 60 sheets (at 1:100,000) for the area include the La Sal (greater Canyonlands area) and Moab (Arches NP) sheets, which are currently in progress (paper and digital format).

Other Sources of Natural Resources Data for the SEUG

The UGS has a significant quadrangle database that they have furnished to NRID for the entire state of Utah.

NRID has compiled a geologic bibliography for numerous parks and monuments, including all parks in the Southeast Utah Group. Visit the website at: http://165.83.36.151/biblios/geobib.nsf; user id is "geobib read", password is "anybody".

SEUG GIS specialist showed a digitized version of Hellmut Doelling's 1985 map as and ArcInfo coverage; attribution needs to be checked; other coverage's should be sought that may exist from the previous GIS specialist

GRD has several entries regarding abandoned mineral land (AML) sites in their database that should be checked for data validity and compared with park records; John Burghardt (GRD) should be contacted regarding this

The Arches NP visitor center sells a publication that has an inventory of all the arches of Arches

The UGS has compiled a CD- ROM with well locations, pipelines, etc. for the state of Utah; GRD should obtain a copy of this. Parks may also desire copies too.

Geologic Hazards

There are numerous issues related to geologic hazards in and around the Southeast Utah Group parks. Below is a brief list of some mentioned during the scoping session:

Landslide and rockfall potential along all roads that occasionally cause road closures; of special note was the problem with the main road in Arches, just above the visitor center

Landscape Arch (ARCH) collapsed in a few places several years ago and was recorded by a tourist

Swelling soils associated with bentonitic shale's of the Chinle, Morrison, and Mancos formations

Radon potential associated with mine closures

Earthquake potential along the Moab Fault

Potential Research Topics for Southeast Utah Group NP

A list of potential research topics includes studies of the following:

What are the connections between gypsiferous rocks and cryptobiotic soils/crusts?; why were the crust healthier on the gypsum- bearing rocks?

How long will Delicate Arch stand?

Engineering studies to determine hazards to visitors; use strain meter

Use High resolution GPS to detect moving, swelling, and collapse in areas of the parks

Rock color studies

Subsurface seismic work for voids in the Needles around synclines and salt dome structures

Locate real unconformity between Entrada Moab Tongue and abutting formations

Action Items

Many follow-up items were discussed during the course of the scoping session and are reiterated by category for quick reference.

Interpretation

More graphics and brochures emphasizing geology and targeting the average enthusiast should be developed. If Southeast Utah Group NP needs assistance with these, please consult GRD's Jim Wood (jim_f._wood@nps.gov) or Melanie Moreno at the USGS- Menlo Park, CA (mmoreno@usgs.gov).

Consider the possibility of hiring a full-time geologist to handle geologic issues for the SEUG; in the absence of this consult with GRD for assistance in geologic matters

UGA Guidebook

Attempt to plant the seeds of this concept to other states for similar publications involving local area geology. Such publications are especially useful for the GRE

Have authors prepare logs that are "sensitive" to delicate areas in the park (i.e. where less user impact is desired)

Paleontological Resources

For now, try to minimize location disclosure of vertebrate sites to minimize disturbances and the potential for theft or vandalism

Develop an in-house plan to inventory, monitor and protect significant paleontological resources from threats; assign staff to oversee especially in regard to the Dalton Wells area

Locate collections taken from the park residing in outside repositories

Geologic Mapping

Attempt to complete digital coverage for the entire SEUG area from existing maps (figure 12)
Locate already existing digital coverage's (like that of Doelling's 1985 Arches map)
Work closely with UGS to finish paper and digital coverage of SEUG area where maps are lacking
Work with cooperators (NABR- Jackie Huntoon) to ensure there work could be incorporated into the master plan of the GRE

Natural Resource Data Sources

Examine GRD databases for AML and disturbed lands for data validity

Attempt to locate other digital coverage's from the previous SEUG GIS specialist (Eric) for Gery Wakefield's (current SEUG GIS specialist) inventory

Miscellaneous

Review proposed research topics for future studies within Southeast Utah Group NP

Promote sensitivity to delicate resources (crusts, etc.) to researchers, and visiting park groups

List of Scoping Meeting attendees with contact information

NAME	AFFILIATION	PHONE	E-MAIL
Joe Gregson	NPS, Natural Resources Information Division	(970) 225-3559	Joe_Gregson@nps.gov
Tim Connors	NPS, Geologic Resources Division	(303) 969-2093	Tim_Connors@nps.gov
Bruce Heise	NPS, Geologic Resources Division	(303) 969-2017	Bruce_Heise@nps.gov
Christine Turner	USGS	(303) 236-1561	Cturner@usgs.gov
Fred Peterson	USGS	(303) 236-1546	Fpeterson@usgs.gov
Jack Stanesco	Red Rocks CC	(303) 914-6290	Jack.Stanesco@rrcc.cccoes.edu
Craig Hauke	NPS, CANY	(435) 259-3911 ext. 2132	Craig_hauke@nps.gov
Grant Willis	Utah Geological Survey	(801) 537-3355	Nrugs.gwillis@state.ut.us
George Billingsley	USGS-Flagstaff, AZ	(520) 556-7198	Gbillingsley@usgs.gov
Vince Santucci	NPS, Geologic Resources Division	(307) 877-4455	Vince_Santucci@nps.gov
Jim Dougan	NPS, NABR	(435) 692-1234	Jim_Dougan@nps.gov
Al Echevarria	Red Rocks CC	(303) 985-5996	Ale44@juno.com
Dave Wood	NPS, CANY	(435) 259-3911 ext. 2133	Dave_Wood@nps.gov
Traci Kolc	NPS, CANY	(435) 259-4712 ext. 18	Traci_Kolc@nps.gov
Margaret Boettcher	NPS, ARCH SCA	(435) 259-1963	Margaret_arches@hotmail.com
Clay Parcels	NPS, ARCH	(435) 259-8161 ext. 245	Clay_Parcels@nps.gov
Alicia Lafever	NPS, ARCH	(435) 259-8161 ext. 242	Alicia_Lafever@nps.gov
Adrienne Gaughan	NPS, ARCH	(435) 259-8161 ext. 286	Adrienne_Gaughan@nps.gov
Shawn Duffy	NPS, ARCH	(435) 259-7223	Shawn_Duffy@nps.gov
Murray Shoemaker	NPS, ARCH	(435) 259-8161 ext. 244	Murray_Shoemaker@nps.gov
Helmut Doelling	UGS	(435) 835-3652	None
Doug Sprinkel	UGS / UGA	(801) 782-3398	Sprinkel@vii.com
Jim Webster	NPS, ARCH	(435) 259-8161 ext. 220	Jim_Webster@nps.gov
Gery Wakefield	NPS, SEUG GIS coordinator	(435) 259-3911 ext. 2180	Gery_Wakefield@nps.gov
Phil Brueck	NPS, SEUG	(435) 259-3911 ext. 2102	Phil_Brueck@nps.gov
Bruce Rodgers	NPS, SEUG	(435) 259-3911 ext. 2130	Bruce_Rodgers@nps.gov
Diane Allen	NPS, ARCH	(435) 259-8161	Diane_Allen@nps.gov
Paul Henderson	NPS, SEUG	(435) 259-3911 ext. 2140	Paul_Henderson@nps.gov

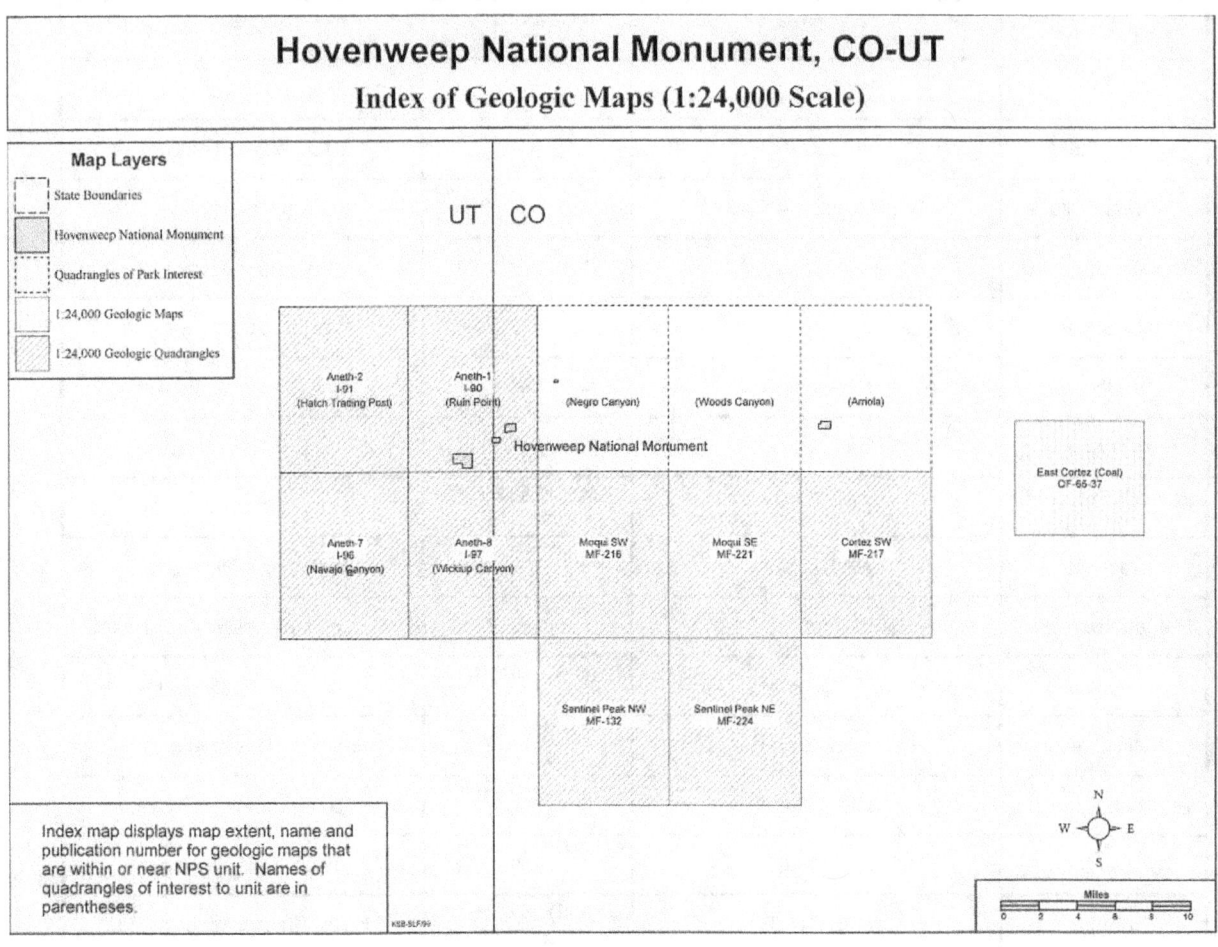

Hovenweep National Monument, CO-UT
Index of Geologic Maps (1:24,000 Scale)

Map Layers

State Boundaries

Hovenweep National Monument

Quadrangles of Park Interest

1:24,000 Geologic Maps

1:24,000 Geologic Quadrangles

UT | CO

Aneth-2
I-91
(Hatch Trading Post)

Aneth-1
I-90
(Ruin Point)

(Negro Canyon)

(Woods Canyon)

(Arriola)

Hovenweep National Monument

East Cortez (Coal)
OF-65-37

Aneth-7
I-96
(Navajo Canyon)

Aneth-8
I-97
(Wickiup Canyon)

Moqui SW
MF-216

Moqui SE
MF-221

Cortez SW
MF-217

Sentinel Peak NW
MF-132

Sentinel Peak NE
MF-224

Index map displays map extent, name and
publication number for geologic maps that
are within or near NPS unit. Names of
quadrangles of interest to unit are in
parentheses.

KSB-SLF/99

N
W E
S

Miles
0 2 4 6 8 10

Figure B.1: Shows map coverage of Hovenweep National Monument at the scale of 1:24,000 and larger. From GRE Scoping Report.

Appendix C: Hovenweep NM Scoping Summary

The following is a summary of the scoping meeting held at Hovenweep National Monument September 5- 6, 2000. This section reflects the views of the geologic inventory and mapping status of the monument at the time of scoping.

Summary

A geologic resources inventory scoping meeting was conducted on September 5- 6, 2000 to discuss how to achieve the production of digital geologic maps for Hovenweep NM (HOVE) units (Square Tower, Holly, Horseshoe Hackberry, Cutthroat, Goodman Point and Cajon). Attendees included the HOVE superintendent, Geologic Resources Division, and GIS staff from MEVE and the Southeast Utah Group.

A geologic resources inventory workshop was held for Hovenweep NM (HOVE) on September 5- 6, 2000 to view and discuss the park's geologic resources, to address the status of geologic mapping for compiling both paper and digital maps, and to assess resource management issues and needs. Cooperators from the NPS Geologic Resources Division (GRD), Natural Resources Information Division (NRID), NPS Hovenweep NM, Mesa Verde NP and Southeast Utah Group were present for the two- day workshop.

Day one involved a half- day scoping session to present overviews of the NPS Inventory and Monitoring (I&M) program, the Geologic Resources Division, and the on going Geologic Resources Inventory (GRI) for Colorado and Utah.

Day two involved a half- day field trip to view the geology of the Hovenweep Square Tower Unit led by Palma Wilson.

Round table discussions involving geologic issues for Hovenweep NM included interpretation, paleontologic resources, and the status of geologic mapping efforts, sources of available data, geologic hazards, and action items generated from this meeting. Brief summaries follow.

Attendees:

Palma Wilson (HOVE Superintendent)
Tim Connors (Geologic Resources Division- GRI_
Steve Fryer (Natural Resources Information Division)
Anne Poole (MEVE- GIS)
Allan Loy (MEVE- GIS)
Gery Wakefield (SEUG- GIS)

Items of discussion included the following:

ProCite database:
Palma Wilson was not aware of a ProCite database for HOVE, but others thought that it could be found in the Colorado Plateau 1994 data that Allan Loy mentioned; needs follow- up.

Geologic Mapping:

The new "Canyon of the Ancients NM" may have new geologic mapping being initiated by the BLM; needs follow- up with local BLM to see if they are producing digital geologic maps of the area and could merge with NPS GRI project.

Anne Poole will be revising the 1950's vintage photo-geologic maps of R.J. Hackman that were never "field-truthed" with field checks to the various HOVE units. Permission will need to be obtained from the superintendent of Canyons of the Ancients (Anasazi Heritage Center at 970- 882- 4811) for the Colorado portion, and from the BLM's Monticello Office for the Utah portion (Kent Walters at 435- 587- 1500).

Anne's main concern is distinguishing the Jurassic Morrison Formation members from the overlying Cretaceous rocks (Burro Canyon and Dakota Sandstone), as she doesn't feel like an expert in that area. Tim Connors has contacted Pete Peterson (USGS-Denver and Mesozoic geologist extraordinaire), who is amenable to working with Anne to give her a better grasp of the stratigraphy. He thought he would be in the area the first week of October and could meet with Anne at that time. More to come when Pete returns from field work.

Anne estimated approximately six months to complete map products (digital finished product) for HOVE.

USGS Map I- 629 (the Cortez quadrangle) has a scale of 1:250,000 and does encompass all HOVE units, but its small scale has shortcomings that 1:24,000 scale mapping enhances.

Digital Geologic Map coverage:
Once the field geology is verified, Anne will be digitizing the entire quadrangles that encompass the HOVE units. She already has four of the quadrangles scanned, rectified and ready for digitization. The others will need to be obtained as topographic maps.

The only units not covered under the Hackman Photo-geologic maps are Goodman Point and Cutthroat. It was also suggested to map the Woods Canyon for continuity and for regional geologic implications. The Square Tower and Cajon units reside in Utah; all the rest are in Colorado.

Quadrangle	HOVE unit
Aneth 1 (aka. Ruin Point)	Square Tower, Holly and Horseshoe Hackberry
Aneth 7 (aka. Navajo Canyon)	Cajon
Negro Canyon	Cutthroat Unit (approximately 14 acres)
Arriola	Goodman Point (1/4 section)
Woods Canyon	none

Paleontology:

Vince Santucci (NPS- FOBU) has indentified paleontological sites within the HOVE units, and needs consulted for this information. It was suggested that a paleontological survey, much like the one being conducted for ARCH, should be done for the HOVE units.

Other GIS data:

Allan Loy is interested in finding out if 10 meter DEM's (digital elevation models) exist for the area; needs follow- up with NRID. It was suggested that Kerry Mich (Intermountain region GIS, Albuquerque) may have some information on this.

Anne Poole is also interested in locating aerial photography used to map vegetation, as it could be useful in mapping the geology; needs follow- up (Mike Story - NRID ??)

Palma Wilson is going to check with San Juan County on their soil mapping activities in the area; needs follow- up.

Interpretation:

During the site visit to the Square Tower unit, Tim Connors suggested that a pamphlet be developed talking about the geology of HOVE along the trail, as the park has a strong geologic component as well as cultural. Tim will attempt to write something up for the park to use to interpret the importance of geology to the HOVE story.

Miscellaneous:

When Anne Poole comes to map, she will need to be in NPS uniform or have the accompaniment of an NPS ranger to avoid conflicts with locals and visitors.

Anne is also interesed in seeing about the availability of park housing while she is mapping the area to cut down on travel time and such; needs follow- up.

The Square Tower boulder foundation has been shown to be eroding and threatening the resource. A report was written on this problem and should be incorporated into a final geologic report on HOVE. Mary Griffitts served as a consultant on this project where the boulders were injected to slow the erosional process. GRD staff were given a copy of the report during the meeting.

Water quality in the area is of concern because of the numerous seeps along geologic units.

Hovenweep National Monument
Geologic Resource Evaluation Report

Natural Resource Report NPS/NRPC/GRD/NRR—2004/002
NPS D-35, September 2004

National Park Service
Director • Fran P. Mainella

Natural Resource Stewardship and Science
Associate Director • Michael A. Soukup

Natural Resource Program Center
The Natural Resource Program Center (NRPC) is the core of the NPS Natural Resource Stewardship and Science Directorate. The Center Director is located in Fort Collins, with staff located principally in Lakewood and Fort Collins, Colorado and in Washington, D.C. The NRPC has five divisions: Air Resources Division, Biological Resource Management Division, Environmental Quality Division, Geologic Resources Division, and Water Resources Division. NRPC also includes three offices: The Office of Education and Outreach, the Office of Inventory, Monitoring and Evaluation, and the Office of Natural Resource Information Systems. In addition, Natural Resource Web Management and Partnership Coordination are cross-cutting disciplines under the Center Director. The multidisciplinary staff of NRPC is dedicated to resolving park resource management challenges originating in and outside units of the national park system.

Geologic Resources Division
Chief • David B. Shaver
Planning Evaluation and Permits Branch Chief • Carol McCoy

Credits
Author • Trista Thornberry-Ehrlich
Editing • Sid Covington
Digital Map Production • Anne Poole
Map Layout Design • Melanie Ransmeier

The Department of the Interior protects and manages the nation's natural resources and cultural heritage; provides scientific and other information about those resources; and honors its special responsibilities to American Indians, Alaska Natives, and affiliated Island Communities.

www.ingramcontent.com/pod-product-compliance
Lightning Source LLC
Chambersburg PA
CBHW080914290526

45795CB00007BA/2520